OF COLOR:
POETS WAYS OF MAKING

an anthology of essays on transformative poetics

Amanda Galvan Huynh & Luisa A. Igloria, Editors

the operating system
print//document

OF COLOR : POETS' WAYS OF MAKING
AN ANTHOLOGY OF ESSAYS ON TRANSFORMATIVE POETICS

ISBN: 978-1-946031-49-5
Library of Congress CIP Number: 2019933115
copyright © 2019, Amanda Galvan Huynh and Luisa A. Igloria, Eds.
edited and designed by ELÆ [Lynne DeSilva-Johnson]
interior layout by Zoe Guttenplan and ELÆ

is released under a Creative Commons CC-BY-NC-ND (Attribution, Non Commercial, No Derivatives) License: its reproduction is encouraged for those who otherwise could not afford its purchase in the case of academic, personal, and other creative usage from which no profit will accrue. Complete rules and restrictions are available at:
http://creativecommons.org/licenses/by-nc-nd/3.0/

For additional questions regarding reproduction, quotation, or to request a pdf for review contact operator@theoperatingsystem.org

This text was set in Minion, Freight Sans, Alegreya Sans SC, and OCR-A Standard.

The front and back covers feature paintings by Suchitra Mattai, courtesy of the artist.
Front: "There's a rain cloud in my garden, if only I had a garden," 2017.
Back: " Plan B," 2017.
www.suchitramattai.com

Your donation makes our publications, platform and programs possible! We <3 You.
http://theoperatingsystem.org/subscribe-join/

the operating system

www.theoperatingsystem.org
operator@theoperatingsystem.org

OF COLOR:
POETS WAYS OF MAKING

2019 OS SYSTEM OPERATORS

CREATIVE DIRECTOR/FOUNDER/MANAGING EDITOR: ELÆ
[Lynne DeSilva-Johnson]
DEPUTY EDITOR: Peter Milne Greiner
CONTRIBUTING EDITOR, EX-SPEC-PO: Kenning JP Garcia
CONTRIBUTING EDITOR, FIELD NOTES: Adrian Silbernagel
CONTRIBUTING EDITOR, IN CORPORE SANO: Amanda Glassman
CONTRIBUTING EDITOR, GLOSSARIUM: Ashkan Eslami Fard
CONTRIBUTING ED. GLOSSARIUM / RESOURCE COORDINATOR: Bahaar Ahsan
JOURNEYHUMAN / SYSTEMS APPRENTICE: Anna Winham
DIGITAL CHAPBOOKS / POETRY MONTH COORDINATOR: Robert Balun
TYPOGRAPHY WRANGLER / DEVELOPMENT COORDINATOR: Zoe Guttenplan
DESIGN ASSISTANTS: Lori Anderson Moseman, Orchid Tierney, Michael Flatt
SOCIAL SYSTEMS / HEALING TECH: Curtis Emery
VOLUNTEERS and/or ADVISORS: Adra Raine, Alexis Quinlan, Clarinda Mac Low, Bill Considine, Careen Shannon, Joanna C. Valente, L. Ann Wheeler, Erick Sáenz, Knar Gavin, Joe Cosmo Cogen, Charlie Stern, Audrey Gascho, Michel Bauwens, Christopher Woodrell, Liz Maxwell, Margaret Rhee, Lydia X. Y. Brown, Lauren Blodgett, Semir Chouabi, J. Lester Feder, Margaretha Haughwout, Alexandra Juhasz, Caits Meissner, Mehdi Navid, Hoa Nguyen, Margaret Randall, Benjamin Wiessner

The Operating System is a member of the **Radical Open Access Collective**, a community of scholar-led, not-for-profit presses, journals and other open access projects. Now consisting of 40 members, we promote a progressive vision for open publishing in the humanities and social sciences.

Learn more at: http://radicaloa.disruptivemedia.org.uk/about/

Your donation makes our publications, platform and programs possible! We <3 You.
http://www.theoperatingsystem.org/subscribe-join/

with

Ernesto L. Abeytia, Melissa Coss Aquino, José Angel
Araguz, Remica L. Bingham-Risher, Ching-In Chen,
Wendy A. Gaudin, Abigail Licad, Kenji C. Liu,
Sasha Pimentel, Khadijah Queen, Tony Robles,
Craig Santos Perez, Tim Seibles, Addie Tsai,
Mai Der Vang, and Ocean Vuong

CONTENTS

Editors' Introductions . 11

Foreword . 23
Mai Der Vang

How Do You Begin? . 26
Ching-In Chen

I'll Take What I Can Get:
Some Thoughts on Erasure Re: MFA vs. POC . 29
Addie Tsai

Holidays: The Custodial Artist as Writer . 34
Tony Robles

On My Grandmother's Face . 39
Wendy A. Gaudin

Reflections on Poetry/Reflexiones sobre la poesía . 48
Ernesto L. Abeytia

Destroyed Out of Her the Great Voice:
On Writing as a Disabled Filipina American Poet . 53
Abigail Licad

Desperate & Beautiful Noise . 61
Tim Seibles

My Life is Not a Stereotype
Though Sometimes Writing About It Feels That Way . 66
Melissa Coss Aquino

On Reading, and Shame . 74
Sasha Pimentel

Becoming the Weather:
Reflections on Poetry as Cultural,
Political, and Spiritual Act . 87
José Angel Araguz

A Radical Poetics of Love
(A Benjaminian Essay on Invisible Man) . 92
Khadijah Queen

Standing in the Shadows of Love:
Desire as Obsession . 101
Remica L. Bingham-Risher

Night Walks:
On addiction, adolescence, and art making . 109
Ocean Vuong

On Writing from Unincorporated Territory . 127
Craig Santos Perez

The Monstrosity: Notes Towards a Frankenpo . 134
Kenji C. Liu

About the book . 140

EDITOR'S INTRODUCTION

Amanda Galvan Huynh

Writing reflects our lives as we understand it in a given present. Upon entering an MFA program, my view of the world told me I had assimilated well. More American than Mexican even though to me the label, Mexican American, takes the form of state-shaped tortillas on my abuela's comal. Dough rolled out into the shapes of Texas, California, Oklahoma, Florida—all imperfect but recognizable. My cultural inheritance: fragmented, yet something I desperately try to stitch back together. I am a child who inherited the fruits of labor from her elders; a child born with the guilt of knowing. Mis abuelos worked the fields of Texas, moved with the season, left pieces of themselves with each harvest, and settled like dirt in Floydada, a rural town that only people with connections to the place can locate on a map.

Tías, tíos, and my parents were pulled from school, or sent after, to work because food on the table meant survival. The repercussions of little education led to low-paying and labor intensive jobs without the opportunity for advancement. For mis primos it meant a myriad of tangents: teen pregnancies, domestic abuse, alcoholism, dropouts, incarcerations, missed opportunities, and making ends meet. Observations of passive violence I've always noted but lacked a vocabulary to explain and express. How does one slip through the cracks? Why does one manage to? At what cost was I standing on someone's back?

In high school, I was one of three Latinx students in the higher-level classes. I learned to dodge the terms "wetback" and "illegal," learned to distance myself from the lower-level Latinx students, learned to quiet my Spanish, and blend in with my surroundings. Survival: denying my heritage and suppressing myself. I had invested in whiteness because overhearing my white math teachers say "Some of these kids are just meant to be our construction workers," filled me with shame. I knew who they talked about; whose skin bore the same color as mine. The lesson on the board: success = white. I carried it with me through college and to graduate school.

In 2014, I entered an MFA Program writing for the white reader by default; I attribute this to six to seven years of lectures from white creative writing professors, critiques by and for the majority of white peers, and the continuous study of white writers. The worst part: I hadn't realized it. While slightly cognizant that I would be better off with professors of color, I did not realize how spot-on my instincts were. Fortune gifted me two professors of color. I wish this sentence didn't need to hold its importance of relief; however, in the landscape of our writing communities it bears witness. What happens when BIPOC writers are given BIPOC faculty? While universities debate the diversity question there are many organizations that have stopped waiting and have started creating the necessary space for BIPOC students and faculty.

In an interview, Sandra Cisneros describes her time at the Iowa Writers' Workshop in the 1970s, her white peers, her professors, and the moment she had her own epiphany:

> *It occurred to me in seminar that we had never—in all my years and education—ever talked about my house. I had seen other houses in literature and media and magazines, but I had never seen my house…and I thought I'm the only person in this room that doesn't have this house… it filled me with a sense of horror and a sense of shame.*[1]

Cisneros's depression turned into anger that fueled her writing. Her four-minute interview gave me permission to be angry, gave me encouragement to transform my frustration into something powerful. Most importantly, it confirmed that I was not alone.

In programs with a lack of diversity, even if there are workshops led by professors of color, the growth of BIPOC writers suffers. NPR's *All Things Considered* covered this in a segment titled "In Elite MFA Programs, The Challenge of Writing While 'Other'" to discuss the challenges of having a supportive faculty, but resistant peers. Justin Torres, former student of the Iowa Writers' Workshop, recounted his hesitation in attending the program as a queer Latinx writer because he would be walking into "a class of middle-class, straight, white people."[2] Automatically, he became othered and his peers resisted his work—which was not the default, which was not white.

To grasp the idea that BIPOC students across the nation in various MFA programs filter the spectrum of microaggressions in an undiversified workshop remains our depressing reality. A handful if not the majority of BIPOC students become discouraged while a few ultimately do not continue. With every BIPOC writer I find similar intersections within our stories: struggle with cultural identity, dissonance within the academe, doubts with being understood, and double consciousness exhaustion. It's almost a miracle that BIPOC are able to survive and graduate with their MFA in creative writing. I know this holds true for me.

Contemporary Classics, a literature class for writers, encouraged us to compile a reading list of National Book Award and Pulitzer Prize winners. In other words, I had to compose a list dominated by white poets. Typically, a student creates their list, finishes their work, and on to the next class. For BIPOC students, we have two options: blend in or stand out. The latter requires extra work, physically and emotionally.

To compensate for the lack of diversity in my first semester, I sought out and read only BIPOC writers. From conversations I have with my BIPOC colleagues and students at other institutions, we are all doing the same thing: searching for voices like our own. I had to search for poets who were writing bilingual poems, who were in conversation with race and identity. Was anyone writing about migrant workers in Texas? If so, how were they creating images? How were they using Spanish? Was the use of Spanish accenting or distracting? What could I learn from them and other Latinx writers? The answer: plenty.

At Old Dominion University's Literary Festival in 2015, I remember my reaction to Manuel Muñoz's reading and my first thought: *that sounds like my abuela*. I recognized something familiar and intimate: my reflection. Later in the year when I read alongside other Latinx writers in Austin the same feeling manifested. Words in English and Spanish coexisted in the same space, and within these stories and poems I felt at home.

Writing bilingual and multilingual poems can provoke numerous debates and discussions; these are also often about craft. What words should be in English and what words shouldn't be? The very existence of bilingual poems pushes against the privilege of "the white imagination...of normality, universality, and transcendence."[3] While publishers and journals are becoming receptive to bilingual texts, the standard format of non-English languages within a text is to italicize, or use other marks to highlight its otherness. But why should we even italicize our bilingual and multilingual experiences? Is it too difficult for readers to imagine our double consciousness?

In my writing, I have had to wrestle with the "italics or no italics" debate, defend my reasoning, and explain my stance and truth: I live a bilingual experience. While a writer using multiple languages would hope that the italics would be the only tough decision, that's not the case. More questions follow: *But what about the reader? What if they don't know Spanish? Isn't the poem lost? Shouldn't you include a translation? What about footnotes?* Of course, the Spanish might be lost on a reader who does not speak the language. I have experienced this in workshop. Naturally, my workshop audience consists of predominantly white students who may or may not take the time to translate. But what are the consequences if I translate my bilingual experience into all English? What is lost? Or really what is at stake if we surrender part of the language that informs our own being?

One night in workshop, I had to critique a white student's poem that used a Latino narrative voice—fast food worker, living at home with his mother, and learning Spanish. Without a doubt, this was the most uncomfortable and frustrating experience. I was told the writer didn't mean any harm. While I'm sure that's true, the reality of the situation is that "unintentionally discriminating is as bad as intentionally discriminating because the result is the same."[4] To be clear, I am not a strong supporter of the idea that everything is fair game in writing. I sit somewhere in the middle of the spectrum as I understand that a writer, regardless of race, should not be boxed into one gender, one race, and so on. However, the poem was only part of the problem. The main issue emerged from the response the poem received from my colleagues and from the writer.

When I, along with another BIPOC student, tried to give advice about the Spanish used, we were discounted because the writer was in the process of learning the "correct" way to speak Spanish. Our experiences and suggestions were not, in that moment, valid. As a workshop group, we did not discuss this situation. For fear of being the angry Latina or overly sensitive student, I kept quiet. It was not until one of our white female students brought attention to it did we even have a chance to communicate the mixed feelings tied to this incident.

Alienation and doubt, during my time in graduate school, were constants with small pockets of air. I have experienced my share of just *being* a writer of color. Some of my encounters I am uncomfortable disclosing while others seem innocuous, but maybe I'm being generous with that term as we are not detached from society as we write. When a peer asked to validate the authenticity of their Latinx character in their story, I questioned my own "authenticity." I do not know the experiences of a Salvadorian, Peruvian, Costa Rican, or any other Latinx heritage besides my own, and I do not feel comfortable speaking on someone's cultural behalf when I can barely write about my own. The idea that I held the key to validate the character left me uneasy because of my own internalized notions that I do not have permission to my own experience because I do not feel "Latinx enough."

The process of writing involves bringing to the page all of our baggage. For myself, it comes with my own internalized racism and classism, and with the realization that "the object of oppression is not only someone outside of my skin, but the someone inside my skin…I have had to confront the fact that much of what I value about being Chicana, about my family, has been subverted by anglo culture and my own cooperation with it."[5] I wish I could disagree with Cherríe Moraga's observations, but I can't because my experience has proven her words to be true. I live in a world where I am forced to be a part of the anglo culture while keeping one foot in my own.

The Latinx experience is multifaceted. However, many who are privileged carry with them the question: "Am I Latinx enough?" It invades everyday life: they either don't speak Spanish well enough, did not grow up in the barrio, can't dance cumbia, don't like spicy foods, or some other "authenticity" ruler. This constant insecurity may be why I hesitate to write about my family's struggles. That underlying fear: am I exploiting my family? There came a point when I had to ask myself if I wanted to continue writing about my family. If I did not write about them then how long would it take for another writer to feel entitled to record their story? The idea makes me queasy because I know it would not be the same as if the writing were to come from someone who lives in and knows the culture's complexities. I do not want to fade into the background. I do not want to be portrayed by someone else. I do not want my family portrayed by someone far removed from the pulse of our lives. So if not me then who?

Naturally, when I became aware of myself my poems and their topics shifted. James Baldwin explains this phenomenon beautifully: "The paradox of education is precisely this—that as one begins to become conscious one begins to examine the society in which [she] is being educated."[6] This new consciousness coexists with the inherited guilt of knowing you are the embodiment of your elders' labor. The reconciliation, for me, happens on the page so when I sit down to write, I ask myself: *What poem did you need? What poem do you need?* If I could relearn creative writing, what types of poems do I wish I was given in the beginning? I imagine my writing would have transformed sooner but trust that it's exactly where it needs to be. It does not stop me from helping emerging BIPOC writers and contributing to our growing community.

What is the benefit of diversity within the MFA? What happens when BIPOC writers have BIPOC mentors? Magic. Conversations around kitchen tables. Ideas born from the nourishment of more than warm bread. It leads to meeting places such as these. A complex compilation of essays as diverse as we are—a beginning.

With a full heart and gratitude, I am thankful to the following poets who have entrusted their essays with us: Mai Der Vang (Foreword), Ching-In Chen, Addie Tsai, Tony Robles, Wendy A. Gaudin, Ernesto L. Abeytia, Abigail Licad, Tim Seibles, Melissa Coss Aquino, Sasha Pimentel, José Angel Araguz, Khadijah Queen, Remica L. Bingham-Risher, Ocean Vuong, Craig Santos Perez, and Kenji C. Liu.

I like to imagine how these words would have shaped me as a green first-year MFA student; I like to imagine how and who they will shape. Even post-MFA I have found pieces of myself in these words. I have reveled in reading these treasures; cheered, cried, and yelled in excitement with each essay. Each one is a revelation into some aspect of our collective being. It has truly been an honor to work with all of you and to take in your light.

To my co-editor Luisa A. Igloria: thank you for saying yes, for running with the idea, for the wonderful guidance on this project, and for being my haven. The list is just too long.

To Amanda Ngoho Reavey, *Tattered Press,* Lynne DeSilva-Johnson, and *The Operating System*: thank you for bringing this anthology into the physical world, and for believing in us and this work.

To BIPOC writers: I hope you find what you need to hear in these pages, the support, the love, the struggle, and the reassurance that you are not alone in this poetic artistry. I hope this anthology will continue the conversation and inspire BIPOC writers who have had a craft book or essays on the backburner to find encouragement to bring these books into the world as we need them as much as we need poems.

Notes

1. Cisneros, Sandra. "The House on Mango Street—Inspiration." Interview by Knopf Group, 1 April 2009.
2. Neary, Lynn. "In Elite MFA Programs, The Challenge of Writing While 'Other.'" NPR: All Things Considered, www.npr.org/sections/codeswitch/2014/08/19/341 363580/in-elite-mfa-programs-the-challenge-of-writing-while-other. 3 October 2013.
3. Rankine, Claudia. "In Our Way: Racism in Creative Writing." The Writer's Chronicle, vol. 49, no. 2, 2016, pp. 47 – 58.
4. Rankine, 51.
5. Anzaldúa, Gloria E. and Cherríe Moraga. *This Bridge Called My Back: Writings by Radical Women of Color.* State University of New York Press, 2015. Print.
6. Baldwin, James. "A Talk to Teachers." October 16, 1963.

EDITOR'S INTRODUCTION

Luisa A. Igloria

There are things I do that I realize I hardly need to think consciously about anymore: when cooking, how to peel and crush garlic and mince ginger; how much vinegar and bay leaf to throw into the adobo; how to rest fingertips lightly on rice grains poured into the pot, and use the second line on the index finger to measure how much water it needs to cook. When sewing a hem, how to pinch two ends of thread together to twirl firmly into a knot. Hearing in my mind *be* (open e)- *a- u- ti- ful* whenever I come across the word beautiful, because that is the way I broke the syllables down in first grade: I turned them into a mnemonic device, to help remember the word for a spelling bee.

What else was I taught, what else did I learn by taste or by feel and remember with my whole body? On certain types of overcast days, the women in my family knew from the look of clouds if there would be mounds of ipon (*sicyopterus lachrimosus*) in the market—wet baskets full of possibly the tiniest fish in the world, their eyes mere pinpricks of black on silvery and translucent bodies. We would coat them in batter and fry them, or steam platefuls in fragrant banana leaves. Before crossing unfamiliar territory or clearing the garden of overgrowth, you were supposed to say to the spirits that you *mean no harm*, and *please may I*. To leave an article of clothing you have worn for a while with the ones you are leaving behind, so the lingering scent of your body might ease their loneliness a little.

My mother was a talented kosturera or seamstress who could rip through a pattern from start to finish in less than three hours, for whoever daughter of some city official had begged to have a dress made at the last minute for a dance or other social event. From her I learned what to me were impossibly sophisticated words like keyhole neckline, godet, eyelet, voile, chiffon, raglan sleeve, facing, piping, placket, ruche, smock, hook-and-eye, frog closure. But when she did not know the names of some colors, I learned it was possible to simply use images or metaphors to substitute for what one did not have the language for: in this way, taupe became *the-inside-of-peanut-skin*. It was even possible to make up a word based on one's memory of how it must have sounded before one forgot what it was—and thus for years, my daughters and I believed my mother when she said *culidon* (not *cartilage*) was the name for the plastic-like, cream-colored connective tissue between bones or that made up the external ear.

None of these were things learned in school. None of these might even be considered useful or logical, in the way that we typically understand what that might mean. But they are the kinds of lessons that have stuck with me the most, and that continue to inform my writing.

My father was of a generation who believed that in order to be "successful" in life, one had to strive to become something of a thinker besides a doer (which seems to imply, though I don't agree, that thinking is somehow the opposite of doing, and vice versa).

At least he believed that one had to develop—especially if one was a girl—a capacity for reflection and self-awareness, besides learning how to do things of a practical nature or with one's hands. Learning to think involved going to school. Not just go to school, but finish school: grade school, high school, college; and beyond that, graduate school. In order to be taken with any seriousness in a world where one was only expected to be pretty and get married, an education would help one to find a job and become "professional."

He thought I would, like him, go to school to study law. Instead, I wanted to make art, something that in my family was not considered practical or serious: *artists are poor, musicians always eat last*. But I wanted to write poetry.

In school, there were plenty of examples of "thinkers," or of individuals who'd lived "the life of the mind." They included philosophers, mathematicians, artists; and inadvertently they were male, and white. The Musée Rodin houses the famous statue "The Thinker." Though the sculpture is cast in bronze, there is no mistaking that its features and physiognomy are European. Despite that, what struck me when I first saw it was how it seemed a depiction of "thinking" as physical, rather than merely austere or coolly cerebral. It was with a kind of shock that I came back to the idea of thought as work, as something that really involves the whole body—and that it was also work to sense things, to feel, to remember.

I was familiar with statues dedicated to the Philippines' national hero, Jose P. Rizal—all the books I read described him as a kind of renaissance man: he was a poet, novelist, doctor, ophthalmologist, polyglot, musician, painter, among other things. In Chicago, where I did my doctoral work in the early '90s, there is a statue of Rizal in a park on Marine Drive, west of Lake Shore Drive. He holds a book in his left hand

and a quill in his right, held just slightly under the chin in that pose again meant to suggest "thinking."

Such a contrast, I thought, to the depiction of Leona Florentino, considered the first Filipina poet to publish in Spanish and Ilokano, and bridge the oral and printed world. Born to a well-to-do family in Vigan, Ilocos Sur, she was married to the town's mayor but was exiled to a different town and shunned by family for the feminist sentiment in her verses. It is also said of her that she fell in love with the woman who was her wine-seller. And yet, her statue in Calle Crisologo depicts a woman in a rather domestic pose—despite a poet's crown of laurel leaves in her hair, she is seated with the traditional striped saya or skirt spread over her thighs and legs and a shawl over her shoulders. She could be a mother or grandmother, eternally waiting at the window for someone to come home—not a poet, not a writer, not obviously a progressive and feminist thinker. I've experienced the difficulty of finding my own models to guide my studies and experience of what it means to write as an immigrant, a woman of color, a person in the diaspora. At the tail end of my doctoral program in the University of Illinois at Chicago, wanting to designate Asian American Literature and Creative Writing Pedagogy as two out of the five sections of my comprehensive examinations, I was hard put to find anyone on the faculty who had the background or expertise in these areas. There were significant primary and critical works, like those of Gloria E. Anzaldúa, Sandra Cisneros, Maxine Hong Kingston, Theresa Hak Kyung Cha, Shirley Geok-Lin Lim, Trinh T. Minh-ha, Jessica Hagedorn, Epifanio San Juan, Jr., Cynthia Sau-ling Wong. But there weren't that many collected works on poetics, theory, or craft for and from the perspective of indigenous poets and poets of color.

Flash forward 23 years for me, to Amanda Galvan Huynh's recent stint as a graduate student in our MFA Creative Writing Program at Old Dominion University. Amanda often came to my office to bewail a similar condition: how she felt that in the craft or theory courses she was taking, there was nothing in syllabi or course reading lists that reflected who she was back to herself. One evening in my kitchen, she finally asked: Have you ever thought of writing a craft book? I admitted that it was something I'd always wanted to do. Before we knew it, we started plotting and planning such a book, and then talking about how to invite others to contribute.

If normative models for learning or thought depict it as mostly separate from the body's functions; and further, as performed in the specialized locale represented by school or the academe—does that extend to poets and how they come to know what they know? For poets of color, what does the relationship of "what one knows" have, with conditions extending but not limited to publishing, mentorship and pedagogy, comradeship and collegiality, friendship, love, and possibility? Is one a real poet if one does not have an MFA? If two poets of color (one male, one female) both teach the same kinds of courses in the same university program, but only one of them is described pejoratively as an "academic poet," what exactly does that mean? For minority poets not considered part of the mainstream because of the combined effects of their ethnic, class, racial, cultural, linguistic, and other identities, what should change in order to accord them the space and respect they deserve? How best can they discuss with and pass on what they have learned to others?

These and other questions come up so consistently in our daily experience as poets of color. And we hear them from poets of color at various stages of their careers. Out of the desire not only to hear from each other but also to share what we've learned—each from our unique as well as bonded experiences of writing as poets of color in this milieu—this anthology project was born.

In this collection, we make no claims of presenting any definitive theoretical or other stance. Neither do we offer these essays as prescriptive of certain ways of thinking of craft or of doing things, although in them is expressed a collective wish—that writers of color find ways to gain strength and visibility without replicating the systems that play the game of divide and conquer and turn us against each other for narrow or self-serving profit. Instead, let there be a steady effort to compile lore and take inventory of strategies, intersections, bridges; to map our histories, to sight possibilities for the future.

We are so honored and thankful to have the words of the following poets in this anthology: Mai Der Vang (Foreword), Ching-In Chen, Addie Tsai, Tony Robles, Wendy A. Gaudin, Ernesto L. Abeytia, Abigail Licad, Tim Seibles, Melissa Coss Aquino, Sasha Pimentel, José Angel Araguz, Khadijah Queen, Remica L. Bingham-Risher, Ocean Vuong, Craig Santos Perez, and Kenji C. Liu.

In lieu of the summary of each poet's essay that is typical in many introductions, I offer here a cento—a prose poem gathering of some lines from their essays, that to me best capture the spirit of what each of us has tried to do for this undertaking:

> *Her father says, "If that's what you must do… then go and do it."*
>
> *Perhaps a new version of literary civility is what we seek, one where poets everywhere, especially those of color, equate the act of writing a poem to starting a fire, if they don't do so already.*
>
> *…may we never stop singing of our elders, ancestors, and every forgotten body that was left behind.*

How do you begin?

To understand this collective story is to understand my own lineage; my body relates to other bodies jostling for breath across time and space.

To be a hybridized body in a predominantly white landscape has everything to do with the choices one makes regarding craft.

Watching his father do janitorial work—custodial work—he learns "No wasted movement, no wasted energy."

I use the essay form to challenge, to unearth, to complicate, to interrogate, and ultimately, to venerate these women and their full lives beyond their phenotypes, beyond their external selves, beyond their condition as the objects of white men's desire.

…poem is about more than a place—it's also about a feeling, a feeling of home and belonging.

If I am to live honestly, with integrity, and believe in my own self-love and acceptance, then I must be comfortable not only with others' discovery of my illness but also with my own declaration of it—unapologetically and without shame.

Why do any of us try so hard to bend the silence, to fashion a voice worthy of a listen?

There is no neutral living. Either our actions significantly reflect our felt sense of things or we perform our lives in spite of what we feel.

For so many of us that target we are aiming for is the tiny space where we manage to tell the truth without enacting stereotypes long used against us, but sometimes our truth feels like a long list of stereotypes no matter which way we turn.

One arrow at a time.

I was ashamed then to feel what stirred in my body. Ashamed to love the dark body.

One must read through their predecessors and the weather their efforts have established, then go against that weather in order to add to it.

To feel is not weakness, but strength. This...advocates for critical engagement based on radical love, rooted in womanist thought. ...[A] poetics of love that works as the opposite of narrowing—

Desire is obsession, the things we keep going back to, that dig in us, that we dig into. Poetry is about mining—extracting things that come back to us—re-examining love and shadows.

The truest ruins are not written down.

The sentence is a linear object—but thoughts are not lines. Memory returns, and to recall is to fill the present with the past. The cost of remembering, then, is life itself.

Are you there? Are you still walking?

My words, they're so still on the page, but on good days, they outpace the bullets.

As a rule, be more.

Write From

Write Oceanic

Write Archipelagic

Write Cartographic

Not an attempt to create a new kind of man, but to grow a monster of compassion and ferocity.

Perhaps only monsters can reinvent humanity, though not with a replacement humanism or dominant universal. Instead, something only monsters, having experienced destruction, can imagine—an ethics of mutual grieving, radical generosity, hospitality.

Thank you to my hard-working co-editor Amanda for her dedication to this project, for her patience, energy, and friendship. And both of us want to thank Lynne DeSilva-Johnson and *The Operating System*, as well as Amanda Ngoho Reavey for making it possible to bring this volume into the world.

FOREWORD

Mai Der Vang

It was an early August morning still hours before any sliver of light, before the surrendering of stars and the turning of a fresh day. In that cavern of familial space seated in the quiet and dimly lit living room at my parents' home, life was beginning to shift. I recall the twist of emotions, feeling as if washed in a sea of anxiety tempered with a strange kind of calm. In a few hours, I was going to board a flight headed to New York City to attend graduate school for an M.F.A. degree in creative writing.

When I heard I had been accepted into the program, I shared the news with my parents though rather vaguely. "You're sure about this?" my father, in his usual stoic manner, asked that day I first mentioned it. He seemed concerned and yet receptive. I was sure. "Well," he continued, "as long as you think you can do it." In that moment, I wasn't entirely sure I could do all of it, leave my hometown of Fresno, end my job at a non-profit youth media organization where I had devoted the last six years of my life, sell my car, and relocate to a metropolis, the opposite of Fresno, in pursuit of a graduate degree that offered no sure return on its investment.

But even in the midst of uncertainty and risk, of endings, beginnings, and reshuffling of life, I knew I had to push on. As a woman of color from an oral culture that has long lacked a definitive literary history, it just seemed there was so much more at stake for me that to *not* do it, to not undertake an opportunity to enrich the possibilities for creative writing in a community largely bereft it, was the real risk. "Yes," I affirmed at last, "I'm doing this."

I grew up in a Hmong refugee family that kept to the ancestral practices of shamanism. It was custom for my parents to conduct a brief ceremony on the day of my departure so the ancestors could lead me on my way. That early August morning, there in the half-light of the living room on the day I would take the first steps into a literary future, I finally began a conversation with my parents about poetry.

"I'm going to study poetry," I said. My parents normally don't meddle in my educational or professional affairs so while I did let them know about my decision to attend graduate school, I hadn't yet shared with them what I intended to study.

"What do you mean poetry?" my mother asked. In searching my thoughts for a Hmong equivalent, I realized we may not have had a definitive history of writing, but we do have a rich oral tradition that includes folk art forms such as sung-poetry. "It's like the *kwv txhiajs* we sing," I explained, "but mine will be written down."

And in this simple conversation, this sudden invitation, this surprising arrival and wild recognition that there must be something larger and more profound ahead, the long-term aspirations I had, to write, to publish, to harness language as a way of pushing against the erasure of our individual and collective stories, to make visible the histories of and traumas suffered by communities like my own, began to spill out of my mouth and into the unexpected space of this moment with my parents.

"If that's what you must do," my father replied, "then go and do it."

He sat down at the kitchen table with lit incense in hand, its smoke trailing the air. It was almost time for me to leave as he proceeded to begin the brief ceremony, which did not require me to be present for its duration. I left there feeling as though a gathering of ancestors were standing alongside me, asserting that while there was a vast universe of work ahead and still so much unknown, the decision to embark on a future of writing was somehow the right one to make.

And this was a choice that not only had the potential to break new ground in my life, for my family, with my community. It would also give me a chance to resound in solidarity with poets of color whose work and presence bring much needed diversity to the national literary landscape, whose voices deepen our understanding and call our care and attention to the lives, experiences, and realities for people of color in this country and throughout the world.

The essays offered in this important collection not only open the heart to feel and be encouraged, they also demand for the ear to hear, to heed, to receive. I am moved by these poets who give of themselves in these essays as a way of honoring each other, their communities, and their shared labor with language. Each of these voices make louder the chorus and drive deeper the rumbling, shape-shifting to become a hand reaching out to touch the reader, as if a mouth has been stitched onto the pages, continually intoning and calling out to say *let us forge our narratives into a new kingdom*. There is at the core of these pieces compassion of the fiercest kind.

That's the kind we desperately need here, now, and today given this country's harsh political climate. There is little time for courtesies or reserved tones. Pleasantries must be discarded in favor of something larger and more truthful enough to echo the frustration and angst felt by so many. Perhaps a new version of literary civility is what we seek, one where poets everywhere, especially those of color, equate the act of writing a poem to starting a fire, if they don't do so already.

And if ever we are told to explain our fire and intensity, to defend our histories of trauma, to clarify our positions of belief, then may we never stop singing of our elders, ancestors, and every forgotten body that was left behind.

Should we be antagonized for our use of native tongues, unrelatable images, syntactical disruptions, or bastardized grammar, then let us answer in the language of stars, in the dialect of rivers, in the vernacular of a rooster's crow.

If ever we are asked why we write, what little room there is for our voices, whether it even matters, then let us return steadfastly to the page.

HOW DO YOU BEGIN?* (ANOTHER POETICS)

Ching-In Chen

Is there someone inside you that you might not have met yet?
— Natasha Marin

Because edges because writing, I am hungry. Chunky beginnings bite outer sections, eating their way closer to detritus. They dream against skin each story.

there is no direct linear trajectory from one narrative fragment, one historical project to the next, and yet when laid side by side, there is a spark between them, the brief connection of synapses necessary to make the impossible connection between body-doubles.

— Larissa Lai

Because Trish Salah, Myung Mi Kim, Natalie Diaz, Maiana Minahal, M. NourbeSe Phillip, Gloria Anzaldúa, Suheir Hammad, Mendi + Keith Obadike, Brenda Cárdenas, Cathy Park Hong, Noah Purifoy, Truong Tran, Douglas Kearney, Catalina Cariaga, Layli Long Soldier, Betye Saar, Juan Felipe Herrera, Akilah Oliver, Kimiko Hahn, Sharon Bridgforth, Sarah Gambito, Craig Santos Perez.

To meet me (a them) is to learn a different syntax, to re-wire your tongue. Do you know my name?

As if the page is a tiny body, a place to practice being alive. And so I'm so curious, still and always, how do trans / genderqueer writers create their textual bodies?

— Morty Diamond

unable to access intimacy to those who lived through this history [excavating the "imagined" and "real" history of xxxx] through a sea of information – dates, locations, numbers – conversing between a historical city existing only in artifacts and an imagined future city re-negotiating its identity through constant redevelopment

Demand concentration, a sinking down past the surface.	*– That you yourself, through recombinations and permutations of the languages you already know, can re-create that fierce charge, for yourself and others, on a page, something written down that remains. – Adrienne Rich*

Using photographs, newspaper articles, maps, scholarly research and archaeological reports alongside dreams and other imaginings, struggling with the erasure of community history and the attempt to reconstruct communal memory through collective acts of re-imagining.

Because I growl from throat, say all variations Remembered, fully present. Monstrous, magnificent, hot-bodied, multi-channeled, blurred cross constraint.	*you can listen to the voice of your other selves * & to the voices of your ancestors * you can push a digit & transfer your voice to image * or vice versa * you don't have to go out anymore * you don't even need to make art or read * our syntax has been simplified to meet your psychocultural needs* – Guillermo Gómez-Peña, Enrique Chagoya & Felicia Rice

Investigating an un-named "shiny city" of the future constantly recycling, cannibalizing, and regurgitating itself, following a traveler as s/t/he/m roam/s through the city before departure.

Because my teeth, my ears, close. Ready to wrestle, waiting for a clearing to take shape.	*... the cyborg does not expect its father to save it .... The main trouble with cyborgs, of course, is that they are the illegitimate offspring of militarism and patriarchal capitalism, not to mention state socialism. But illegitimate offspring are often exceedingly unfaithful to their origins. Their fathers, after all, are inessential.* – Donna Haraway

These two "cities" reflections of each other, continually in the process of un-making and re-making themselves in the imagination of those connected to them through their layered trails of artifacts and the stories that surround them.

In a conventional novel readers expect to be told – what happens to {   }? Is she a reliable source of her story? Who is she in any one moment and how can we trace who she has become by the end of the novel? A progression is demanded. Has she moved forward or backward? Are her movements intelligent?

Because of course – we are all human etcetera. Call it woman, call it queer, call it non-conforming, call it different color, accent (or less), set apart from its family container.   If my bodies profit prison, ship carrying laborer hands, moneyed network financing servitude, secret name swallowed into tongue, it/they/we exist/in uneasy relation.

– Laynie Brown

To understand this collective story is to understand my own lineage; my body relates to other bodies jostling for breath across time and space.

Because to never feel whole
grow the landscape in front of us.
Mouth open and loose waits.

My Uncle Eng once asked me if I understood the work of a writer. I told him that a writer writes stories, with beginnings, middles, and ends. He shook his head. He told me, "A story is like the stop sign on the road of life. Its purpose is to make you stop, look both sides, check the trajectory of the horizon before you continue. Until you understand this, you are not yet a writer."

– Kao Kalia Yang

[Note: * from **Bhanu Kapil's** *The Vertical Interrogation of Strangers*]

I'LL TAKE WHAT I CAN GET: SOME THOUGHTS ON ERASURE

RE: MFA VS. POC

Addie Tsai

To that end we should remember that it is the 'inter' — the cutting edge of translation and negotiation, the inbetween space — that carries the burden of the meaning of culture. . . . And by exploring this Third Space, we may elude the politics of polarity and emerge as the others of our selves

– Homi K. Bhabha

By the time I graduated with a Bachelor of Arts in English with a concentration in Creative Writing, I could not say that I had the tools or the lineage to understand the particular position I occupied as a poet of biracial identity. As a child of an omnipresent and abusive Chinese father, a weed-addled and abandoning mother, it was enough in those days to survive. I was desperate for any male (or female) figure to hold onto. I took in stride the little cuts regarding the ways in which my racial background entered my poems—such as the time that my poem "Ode to Rice" was literally mocked in an all-white workshop led by a white male graduate student: *tomatoes aren't Asian, this poem should include Asian stuff, like lemongrass and soy sauce*, or *wouldn't it be fun if this named all the different brands of rice, like Uncle Ben's rice, or Minute rice*, etc. I did not know how to fight for anything other than mockery or condescension. It wasn't so much that I merely went along with the idiosyncratic way that any material I brought into a workshop was mocked or derided, it was that, at that age, at that time, I expected it. I took what I could get, where I could get it. When the white male poet who I still refer to as my mentor—the first poet to take me under his wing, to praise my talent, to push me in places that were hard to travel on the page—sat me down at lunch in the campus cafeteria and told me, point blank, that I needed to make sure my first manuscript of poetry addressed my *Asianness, because without being in a workshop, no one will know that you aren't white*, I felt tokenized, but at the same time not in a position to refute the kindness of strangers.

For, truth be told, that kindness was more than I had ever received from my parents. Who was I to look a gift horse in the mouth?

Many times I scrawled what I imagined would be the opening sentence of my first memoir: *I am like that overlap in a Venn diagram, pug nose and almond-shaped eyes, their hazel tones giving me away, neither one nor the other.* I felt it was no less than a miracle when I learned that I was accepted to the low-residency program I would soon attend, a program I learned of from other white poet faculty and graduate students in the program where I received my Bachelor's. I felt like a fraud among Asians, for my father had kept me from any true immersion in that world; and although I certainly didn't feel I could authentically exist in a white universe, I was still naïve enough to believe that if I played the game sincerely enough, I wouldn't be forsaken.

Although I can say without doubt that my experience in my MFA absolutely changed me and transformed my relationship to craft in a profound way, I was also transformed by the ways in which I felt my body as a poet of color erased, made invisible, or more to the point, explicitly directed to change course so as not to make the white bodies—both students and faculty—uncomfortable with my foreignness.

I pushed and fought and toiled in my own way. I continued to insert Chinese characters into the text of my poems, even when I was told repeatedly by the almost all white body of students in any workshop that I needed to translate them in footnotes, even when the character was followed with a literal translation, even when other poems which included any of the Romantic languages—Italian, French, Spanish, German—left their incomprehensible texts to stand without explanation. I continued to argue, to question, to implore what it was about my particular non-white body that made my poetic material so difficult. I didn't understand the characters I was inserting into the poems any more than others did. But it was this push of meaning and language, this representation of my interior and exterior life as one who was surrounded by Mandarin but without any tools to understand those sounds, that I wanted to explore, and that I wanted acknowledged by my peers and by my mentors. It seems almost ironic that by the time I would finally meet faculty of color, I was either kept from them by yet another white male faculty enforcing his way into working with me instead, or being connected with two new Asian faculty just as I was reaching my essay-long semester project, which left almost no time for any engagement with my creative work.

I discovered just how white this MFA program was, ironically, during the lecture a faculty of color gave during my second residency. The name of the lecture was titled *Sven! Without your dashiki I hardly recognized you!* Perhaps that should have alerted me to what might happen within the next hour, but most of the time I spent in the heady rush of learning, and took all substance that I could gather from whatever it was I experienced there. Although I became immediately embroiled in the entire context which this faculty member had set up for a mostly white student and faculty body, it was, in reality, the responses to the set up that absented me, quickly and painfully, from the room. If memory serves, and I believe it does, the game was called *Name the Colored Person*. The faculty member then proceeded to read short excerpts from various writers of color. The students (or any other faculty in attendance) were to, quite literally, name the "color" of the piece.

At first, I thought to myself, *this must be a joke, this can't actually be happening*. But, oh, it was. The answers that proceeded were the most horrific, tone-deaf answers I had ever witnessed with regards to othered bodies: *That one's Asian because foot binding. That one's Jewish because overbearing mother.* And onwards it went. It began to feel like assault, an erasure of trauma enacted upon bodies of color by white interpreters for centuries. For the first time, I felt myself leave the present moment as it continued, and I surveyed the lecture hall of bodies that surrounded me, bodies who I felt understood me, with whom I felt safe. It was then I realized I was the only student of color in the entire genre. There was a single Asian student in all of the fiction genre as well. There was one faculty member of color in poetry, who had been invited for the first time, and two in fiction. This lecture had initially been the reason I pushed myself forward, although incredibly shy, out of admiration, to connect with this poet. Thankfully, we were able to have the conversations I could have with no one else, that got me through the myriad realizations I was having about my position in the program, and the ways in which my body was disavowed there.

Although it would be easy to say that I wished that entire experience never took place, it helped me understand the ways in which bodies of color can, even if largely unintentionally, become tokens of racial inclusion, in institutions that aren't able to understand what else needs to be acknowledged. It's been over ten years since I attended the program, and in the time since, the program's inclusion of faculty and students of color (as well as intersectional identities such as queer students of color) seems to have evolved a thousand-fold. I was told by a student at the most recent reunion at a writing conference that a number of them got together and took their grievances regarding diversity to the powers that be, and over time, their complaints were addressed. Sometimes it takes a group to inform change. I regret that, ultimately, I had been too passive to make any real demands, too cemented in my psychology still as a child abuse survivor to know how to push against the institution that allows such erasure, rather than taking what I could get.

I did attempt to push against the institution with regards to underhanded policies regarding people of color. At my third residency, I was paired with a poet of color whose work had been tremendously impactful during my undergrad: the first contemporary biracial Asian poet I'd heard read in person. It was time to work on my semester-long essay project, a 30-50 page analytic essay that demonstrates how an "expert" in the genre manages a particular set of craft elements. I wanted to study an Asian American poet who particularly informed my creative work at the time, Li-Young Lee. Other poets I had on the initial list that I retrieved from my files: Mei-Mei Berssenbrugge, Amy Kwan Berry, Rick Barot, Cathy Song, Chitra Divakaruni, Marilyn Chin, and Paisley Rekdal. I was beyond thrilled that, at long last, I was working with a biracial Asian American poet; it seemed a perfect opportunity to more deeply understand the ways in which Asian American poetics address identity via craft.

I was told, explicitly, that I was not allowed to use any of these poets. It became such an "issue" that I was taken into a private meeting with the director of the program, where I was told that for an essay of this magnitude, they would like us to focus on poets that are clearly "experts," and that many of these poets simply didn't have enough book publications to warrant that title. After the meeting, I walked silently past all the students who could bask in the sun, comforted by their visibility and recognition. I tucked myself into a ball on the plastic mattress in my dorm room and wept. It seemed my squeaky small presence on the audible mattress was a perfect metaphor for how the policing of which text I could use in my essay ultimately policed my own body and politic in the program as well. As Junot Diaz states in his *MFA Vs. POC: Simply put, I was a person of color in a workshop whose theory of reality did not include my most fundamental experiences as a person of color—that did not in other words include me.*

This is what I did not have the heart or agency to explain to the degree-conferring bodies of my institution: you cannot remove the role of patriarchal whiteness from any aspect of their judgment that the poets on my list were not experts because they hadn't published enough in order to be deemed experts. And this had everything to do with the fact that they were not me, forced to write in and continue to contribute to a textual body of whiteness. Secondly, what this decision also made invisible was the relationship a person's otherness (or whiteness) had to do with how one crafted their own poetics. To be a hybridized body in a predominantly white landscape has everything to do with the choices one makes regarding craft.

By the end of the residency, the program had given me a consolation prize: I would get to write about Derek Walcott, a Caribbean poet, rather than Robert Frost. Although I learned a great deal from Walcott with regards to how he expanded the romantic lyric with his fragments of landscape and the patois formed from the colonialist burden of the island, I always wonder what I would have come away with if I had been offered a place in which to discover my own truth, rather than consoled with the kind of writer of color they were willing to read about. It seems telling that when I look back at my reading list of that time, not only was it filled to the brim with white writers, but that almost every one of them was presently, or had been in the past, a faculty of the program.

In my final residency there, I would no longer ask for permission. I worked with a poet who did not claim to understand me at the start, but who asked for me, quite clearly, to offer any information that could help her understand from where the work emerged. So, I decided that I would study three biracial Asian American poets' use of the image in their work for my final graduation class presentation, arguing that their poetics were as hybrid as their bodies were. It was completely a non-issue. It wasn't even a thing that I would get to do. It came without question, without a private meeting, without a curled body on a sunken couch. I have learned, over time, that resistance generates change; or at the very least, a way out of the self-policing and instead to self-materialization.

HOLIDAYS: THE CUSTODIAL ARTIST AS WRITER

Tony Robles

I remember long ago my introduction to the holy trinity. My father made the introduction. He was not a religious man. He inched his way towards the house of worship—the Catholic brand—at the untimely (or timely) death of a friend or loved one or perhaps Easter. He would sometimes regale me—a kid of 11 or 12—with tales of some of the goings on in the church. "There's lots of punks in the priesthood," he'd say, alluding to the penchant priests had for young boys—recalling his own visit to a parish priest as a boy in search of a job. "Well, son, let's have a *look* at you," said the priest, who made my young father stand in the middle of the room. "Turn around," said the priest, "A little bit more to the left…ok, now bend over."

"What did you do?" I asked my dad. "What the hell you think I did?" He'd reply. "I got the hell outta there"—showing wisdom beyond his years in knowing that such an encounter with the pristine collar would put him in quite the motherfucking wringer. In *getting the hell outta there* he proceeded, in quick fashion, to go to the restroom where he proceeded to climb out of the nearest stained-glass window. He wove such tales while on the couch or driving his brown Cutlass with the tan roof on Van Ness Avenue past the Opera House, the place that employed him as a janitor. That grey edifice wielded much influence on his life as the church. The building, whose walls contained the voices of world class sopranos and tenors, pop vocalists, and a myriad of other artists also held the sounds my father made—a janitor, a custodial artist of the highest order. I think of him and my introduction to the holy trinity—an introduction that still amazes me and that led me to become a writer.

I think of my father as I make my way to City College of San Francisco where I have been invited to speak to a morning English class. I have received an increasing number of requests for such presentations since the publication of my book of poems and short stories—*Cool Don't Live Here No More—A Letter to San Francisco*. The poems and short stories, offering goofball insights gleaned over the last 3 decades of my life in my city—firings, epiphanies of a solitary nature, the eviction crisis, the decay of the city spirit, not to mention various wisecracks—have gone over quite well with readers; for the first time in my life, people appear genuinely interested in what I have to say. I take the same bus I used to take when I attended this institution more than 2 decades ago. I get off the bus and see the buildings—so much a part of my life when I had no idea where I would end up—a chair or perhaps on land, sea or air—I had not the faintest idea. With stumbling innocence I walked the halls to my classes, to the bathroom, in search of something or in the quest to convince myself I was in search of the ever elusive *it*.

I roam the halls some 20 years later. I see the same floors, doors, structures—new and old—incubators of dreams, thoughts, disappointments, heartbreak—the collective tissue of the human experience. I see the faces of aspiring artists in the Creative Arts building, sitting on the floor with sketchbooks and boards, waiting for class, waiting for inspiration as droves of their fellow humans pass by in either direction in a runway procession which is the hall. I find, in my search for the classroom that awaits me that I am in the wrong building. I am directed to the correct building by a kindly art teacher. I finally arrive at the classroom. It is nearly full with students, some sitting, some arriving.

"Mr. Robles?" a voice announces. I am not accustomed to such formal introductions. I am more accustomed to *Hey! What do you want? Can I help you with something?* or, most commonly: *You must have the wrong place.* "Mr. Robles?" Who might this person be? In a lifetime of encounters with the mirror I am still half unsure of who it is I see on the other side. Mr. Robles, I say under my breath as I look and search for my father.

Getting back to the holy trinity: I became acquainted with this bell curve trifecta via janitorial work—the daily duty endured by my father to keep a roof over my head and food in my gut. Perhaps this trinity possessed a spiritual quality as engendered by the church and its texts. There is a father and son—a division of labor that is one and the same. In that, we have a commonality or affinity, may I dare say, to the divine. However, the trinity of which I speak is much more tactile to the senses of those of us who are sentient beings. The trinity that my father so deftly introduced me to was the bucket, the mop, and the wringer. What, you may ask, do these items or implements have to do with an academic setting, or anything of any consequence whatsoever?

My father, as custodial artist, likely never thought of himself as an artist, or a custodian. The custodian title was bestowed upon him as a result of circumstances permeating his life. He came of age at a time when opportunities for young men of color were very limited. The limitations imposed reflect more on the limitations of the institutions themselves and the moving—that is—human parts that make them function. But my father was an artist. That is not to say a formally trained artist, but art and expression moved in his blood. Let me communicate to you that he was an artist from the moment he rose from bed to the moment he showered to the moment he put on his shoes. His mundane movements, his moving from point A to B was a dance, a flow, an exhibition of a story imparted to him that lived in his bones and moved across his skin like the songs that kept us alive, filling our empty pots with something that would sustain us when we could barely look into the mirror to confront who we were. In the expanse of his dreams sprinkled with Horatio Alger notions and delusions, he started his own janitorial business—a 2-man crew—he and I in an attempt to climb the socioeconomic ladder for him and a baptism of fire for me.

In the name of the bucket, mop and wringer: I am in the classroom with a respectability gleaned over time, glistening with the patina of failed efforts and requisite idiocy that plagues those of us blessed by the human condition—a C+ average student who managed to somehow make it. But I remember myself before I became Mr. Robles, before I became this scribe, this imbiber of words—in short, I recall myself when I wasn't shit—no title, neither Mister nor author, fish nor fowl or otherwise. I look at the faces about me, not unlike my face 20 years earlier when I walked face first into the walls of this hallowed institution searching for direction. I remember sitting in classes, writing my name on endless sheets of paper, scribbling quickly—barely knowing the meaning of my name—that is—the meaning of my life. Hours in the typewriter lab pecking away at the keys like some hungry bird too burdened to fly. "Mr. Robles," I hear again. And just as quickly as it is said I find myself in a room with my father. It is a room not unlike the classroom I am visiting—roughly the same dimensions. I see his face. It is riddled with urgency and impatience.

"Hey, step on it!" he says.

"Step on what? I'm an author."

"Well, you might be an author but you ain't shit when it comes to mopping a floor. Look at that floor…does it look clean to you?"

I look at the floor. It glistens and the air is heavy with the scent of industrial floor cleaner whose aroma burns the nostrils. "I don't see anything wrong."

My father looks at me as if I have lost my mind, and perhaps I have.

"Look at that," he says, running his finger over an area of the floor. "You missed this."

I look at the area and he is correct, I missed a few spots. "The mop must have…"

"Oh, it's the mop's fault?" my father says. I look at my father. His dust rag hangs from his back pocket, his key ring brazen with a dozen keys dangling from his belt loop. His mind is moving in pace with his body. His eyes notice everything, every speck on the wall, every fly on the wall documenting the event.

"Those are holidays," my father says.

"What's a holiday?"

"It's when you mop a floor and you miss spots. You never want to have holidays. I thought I taught you better than that. You disappoint me."

"But…"

"But *my ass*. This was supposed to be a simple operation…*boom boom, in and out*. Now instead of finishing the job we have to backtrack over your half-assed work. We could be eating hamburgers and french fries right now but instead we're going over your work."

"I like hamburgers."

"For the half-assed job you did on this floor, I wouldn't give you a packet of ketchup. If anything, you deserve a foot in the ass. Mop the floor again—wait, better yet—let me do it. Keep your eyes open and your mouth shut. Learn something."

I watch my father wring out the mop and glide it over the floor. Wide strokes, cutting at the corners in a loop, a rhythm ensuing that is part music, part urgency, part dance that—when added together—gets done what needs to get done. No wasted movement, no wasted energy.

"See, that's how it's done," my father says. I look at the floor. Every inch mopped over, no holidays to be seen. "Now go and take care of the toilets and let's get the hell outta here."

I needn't belabor the point that when one encounters a toilet, particularly one in a public space—especially when you have been entrusted with the maintenance and cleanliness of said toilet—that your encounters with the shit stain are inevitable. The quality or tenor of these encounters can be measured by any number of factors—not the least of which is the mood or state of mind of the one wielding that spiritual baton a.k.a. the toilet brush. In my case, the scrubbing ensued. I worked up quite a sweat with my toilet brush: a back and forth frenzy reminiscent of a club DJ scratching a record, creating rhythms and sounds he didn't know he had. The shit stain was stubborn—as shit stains usually are—and the more I scrubbed, the more the porcelain seemed to mock me. Mind you, this is only one variety of shit stain, as many more varieties exist, in one manifestation or another—oftentimes in the form of other persons, who are far more difficult to make disappear.

"Don't take all day on that toilet," my father calls out. I scrub until my eyes hurt. I not only scrub the shit stain in the porcelain bowl but, with my effort, attempt to scrub the shit stain of the world, the shit stain that smears across the mind, the shit stain that clouds the imagination and begets more shit stains. My assault is not for naught as my father inspects my work and announces that I'm finally getting the hang of it, that I—if you will—halfway have my shit together. But this is temporary relief, for the shit stain does not retreat into obscurity for long, but makes consistent and at times cameo appearances in the form of family, friends, and neighbors. So, while my father laments "holidays" on a mopped floor, one can never hope for a holiday from the shit stain. An ever bigger quandary comes when in the process of scrubbing the toilet you realize that you, at that moment, must utilize it. But this is another topic for a future essay. I help him load our janitorial supplies in the van before taking off for a hamburger and more father and son dialog.

"Mr. Robles?" A voice says. I look around the classroom. I learned much within the walls of this institution yet I cannot extricate myself from my father—for he was the one who taught me most about what would ultimately become my craft: writing. When telling me, "Don't leave any holidays," he was speaking of the lines that I would eventually attempt to write. Thorough and fluid, his mop strokes were lines, were art—communicating an intention that lived in his core that would not accept anything less than the truth. "Don't leave holidays" could easily mean, do not lie, do not deceive, do not take for granted the time or attention of your reader. He was truly my first editor, spotting my omissions, flaws and holidays.

I rise from my chair, ready to impart to these students my story and, hopefully, some inspiration in relating my experience as a poet; that is, a teller of truth that only the poet can report and is bound to report just as he or she is bound to breathe. Don't leave any holidays, I whisper to myself as I rise to speak before this class. The class gleams with everything my father taught me as I have the students' undivided attention.

ON MY GRANDMOTHER'S FACE

Wendy A. Gaudin

We called our grandmother *Mema*. Here is how you say her name: accent on the *me*, not the *ma*; open-mouthed *ma*, not slack-jawed *maw*; slightly nasal timbre throughout. Say it brightly, as if the sun were shining into your mouth as you speak: *Mema*. Say it in a way that makes your teeth show, a smiling expression: *Mema*. Say it with your eyes wide open, face tilted up to the sky, like you were calling her name from your roller-skated feet, up on the corner of Key West and Los Alimos, your dark brown and heavy braids striking both sides of your waist, their rubber band and index finger-curled ends like weights at the termination of a long fishing line, and she is on the corner of Bismarck Avenue, within your sight, standing in front of your golden home with its delicate, dichondra grass and olive tree, she: in her fuzzy slippers and ubiquitous housecoat.

Mema lived in a bungalow on the west side of the city of Los Angeles, a mountain range and two freeways away from my home in the San Fernando Valley. You can picture it in your mind: a little blue and white house, with a raised, gated porch and a breakfast nook with angled windows that looked out onto the street. A canary yellow kitchen table with matching chairs, a teal and white paisley couch under a thick plastic cover, and a lamp with a miniature piano as its base sitting on a circular table with one curved drawer and one leg that spread out into three. On the back porch, there was an antique washing machine, with its handle and twin rollers and big bucket, and in the back yard, a clothes line, beets and collards, mustards and radishes.

Her house had two bedrooms tucked in the back like carrots buried under the earth. The one on the right was her room, and it had its own powder room and dressing table complete with a mirror and an upholstered stool. The Virgin Mary and the Immaculate Heart of Jesus hung framed on the wall above her bed, whose white chenille bedspread made a bumpy feeling under my hands when I ran them over it. A Kleenex box on a dresser held her stash of 100 dollar bills. A gas heater warmed the bathroom, and the porcelain tub included a rubber plug at the end of a chain.

Her bathroom smelled like pine Airwick, the kind that was like a wet spongy stick suspended in brightly-colored liquid, and you pulled the stick out of the bottle to spread the smell.

The bedroom on the left was Pop's. Pop was Augustus Lawrence Burns, the grandpa that I never met. Mema kept his door closed, and when I entered his room, it was very cold and, I always thought, it smelled of him. With the boxes of unopened gifts hidden under the bed, and everything in a state of unmovement, it felt like a dead person's room. When I slept at Mema's house, I started out in Pop's cold double bed, a copy of *Valley of the Dolls* on the nightstand, but I ended up cuddled up beside Mema in her bed, with a strawberry blonde Jesus watching over me.

On the walls, you might find a large photograph of a young Mema with her son, Sonny Boy, when he was just a small, brown-skinned child. You might see a framed photograph of Pop, wearing a plaid shirt and horn-rimmed glasses, wavy grey hair and a moustache, his eyes looking away from the camera. You might see one of those painted photographs of Mema herself at an older age, a strand of pearls around her neck, her shoulders painted narrower than they should have been, her dark hair swept up in a pile on top of her head.

Mema had no photographs of the family that came before her, the people from whom she came. No images of her mother, her father, her grandparents, her sister Marguerite, cousins, extended family. If you entered her bungalow at 3215 West 30th Street, with its castle motif and semi-circular windows, you might wonder where she came from. How did she get here, with her white-white skin and cornflower blue eyes, gelatinous, homemade hogshead cheese in a glass dish in the refrigerator, a crystal rosary and a saint's medal in her purse, her accent and grammar from some other place? Her face: an opus. A sand mandala. A grand sequoia in a serene California wilderness, a face telling its whole history, its movements and its arcs, its crescendos and its abbreviations, the rich and full inheritance of the Mississippi Valley and the parts that were missing, all of it calling me back. To Louisiana.

*

I arrived in New Orleans a returnee, a backslider, a backward-settler of sorts, most definitely out-of-sorts with the accents of this place, the colloquialisms, the hierarchical titles and local manners, and I didn't have to announce myself: the tone of my voice did it for me, my pronunciation, my reformed-Valley Girl enunciation, the way that I carried my body, the way that I directed my gaze, the way that I wore my hair: naturally curly, windy and swirly, unpressed, unrolled, unrelaxed, untreated, unfixed, untamed, un-done-something-with. The only thing that marked me as somehow part of this place was my very Southern Louisiana surname. Gaudin.

In 1930, Mema and Augustus Lawrence Burns—he, working as a Pullman Porter, she, listed as a laundress in the 1929 New Orleans *City Directory*—boarded the Sunset Limited bound for Santa Monica, California. Their first daughter they left behind. Mema held Sonny Boy in her arms. My mother was born almost a decade later. They were the earliest among the thousands of Louisiana Creoles who later left their homes, traditions, foodways and families behind to embrace a new life in sunny, Southern California, where the streets were paved with gold, where black people sat at the front of the bus, where their racial classification was ambiguous at best but their ethnicity as Southern Louisianans was clear as the bright blue sky as soon as they opened their mouths.

My return to this place was a reclamation of history and ancestry. And privilege. My ability to return at all signals my family's positioning as those who could and did choose to leave.

I lived on the bottom floor of a double-gallery up on Laurel Street, where the floats, marching bands, and hooded men on horseback gathered and lined up before Carnival parades. An old Hinderer's iron fence lined the tiny front yard and banana trees leaning heavily against the rotting wooden fence in the back. My mother came to visit me, and we drove up the river road to the little town of Vacherie where Mema grew up, encircled on one side by tall, perennial sugar cane tresses and on the other side by the serpentine levees of the Mississippi River. Walking through the cemetery behind Our Lady of Peace, we spotted the headstone of Mema's Aunt Ella. In the central library in downtown New Orleans, on the third floor in the Louisiana room, we found Mema's father in the obituary of the *Times-Picayune*.

There he was: survived by his wife and his two sons, his eight grandchildren, and his seven great-grandchildren. No mention of a daughter. My mother stood peering at the microfilm. *Wow,* she exhaled, *there he is.*

The short story that Mema had told was this: her father was a French doctor. She didn't know him as her father, only as the person who fathered her, under circumstances unknown, marking her as a child born outside of wedlock in a Catholic family, in a Catholic community, in a place with a long history of mixed race women giving birth to the children of white men. She saw him only once: her mother took her to the hospital where he worked, and when he walked by, Mema's mother uttered the stark words: *There's your father. Now you've seen him.*

*

After my mother returned to her California desert home, I continued my search for my great-grandfather, the name alone connoting warmth. A sweet old man. Reverence. Origins. Offerings. *Great-grandfather*. In our family history, the term is clinical. Literal. Cold.

According to the obituary, he was born in New Orleans in 1882, both of his parents also French-named, both of them born in New Orleans. He attended McDonough Sixteen primary school, Warren Easton secondary school, and Tulane University, where he graduated with a medical degree. His specialization: obstetrics and gynecology. Irony of ironies.

Learning this last bit of information, I headed to Tulane University's archives. I began with the *Jambalaya*, the university's annual, and with very little time or effort, I found him among the other graduates of the Medical Class of 1904: all presumably white men, all but a small number wearing dark suits and ties, sporting large mustaches and squinting in the sun. Although it would be impossible to find him in this large group, I have narrowed my search down to two faces: on the right at the top, one man with thick, dark hair, head turned, and another man in the front, far left, with lighter hair and fading out of the photograph. But he really could be anyone in the image. And, really, all of them could be he: white boy growing into a white man in the Deep South, white man with an endless vista, an endless number of open doors, an endless number of women of color to sample like hors d'oeuvre except with brutality, with impunity, shielded by anti-miscegenation laws, anti-cohabitation laws, anti-concubinage laws, racial integrity laws, shielded by laws that made their offspring rumor, that made their sex recreational, that made their children *quadroons*, like light-skinned knickknacks arranged on a shelf, laws that made their progeny illegitimate. He could be any of them, all of them.

While I was flipping through the aged pages of the *Jambalaya*, an archivist handed me a file with his name on the front. *Graduate faculty of Medicine, 1924-1948*. Opening it, I found him – his face, in sepia, staring at me staring at him: his head slightly angled to the right, his straight, light-colored hair beginning at his widow's peak, frameless glasses sitting high upon his long, narrow nose; cornflower blue eyes, thin lips, a dark suit with a silky tie tucked into the vest, and ears with dangling lobes. I looked through his file and learned his entire personal and professional history: his home addresses, his clinical appointments, and his connection to Vacherie: from 1904 until 1910, he practiced medicine in the little town on the Mississippi River, where Mema's maternal family had lived for over 100 years.

*

I went home to Laurel Street and stuck a tack through my copy of the photograph of my great-grandfather, and pushed it into the corkboard above my desk. Next to him, I tacked a copy of a photograph of my great-grandmother, whom her family called *Touse*, the same woman he had his way with sometime in the month of July, 1904. History manuscripts, census records, university files, diocesan records, and obituaries helped me form an outline of the story of Mema's birth and her life as one of a countless number of fatherless children of white men, but so much was missing. So I turned to poetry not only to delve into the narrative of Touse and the doctor with the cornflower blue eyes, but also to tell their story through mine, which are not blue but brown with bits of green when the sun shines into them.

> *I saw you*
> *posing with forty-six men and one woman in an old yearbook*
> *a hat in your hands, in profile*
> *dark suit and tie like the other faculty*
> *you are half-smiling and resting one foot on a step*
> *and you don't look like the cactus we had been expecting*
> *alien flesh and sharp to the touch*
> *but my mother says that you don't look happy.*

Through poetry, I contemplate the entire dilemma of fatherhood in Mema's life. For example, the moment that Touse's mother learns of her young daughter's pregnancy:

> *I imagine her in stiff black shoes*
> *and an apron around her waist*
> *okra seeds and shrimp antennae stuck to her hands*
> *when she came looking for you*
> *to unbury your private little act with her daughter*
> *like a little white potato or a tuber root*
> *cold in the ground:*
> *so much potential*
> *when the soil is brushed away...*

and the plain fact of my grandmother's existence:

> *...you are newlywed and forgetting*
> *when she gives birth:*
> *it's a girl child*
> *with blue eyes and a sharp nose*

> *fair hair and a turned-down mouth*
> *and everyone knows she is your child*
> *but no one says it out loud.*

I consider my great-grandfather, himself, as a child:

> *I am sure McDonough Sixteen's yellowed annuals*
> *would show you with a head full of hair*
> *small turquoise eyes and blond lashes*
> *still diaphanous*
> *and grown-up clothes to make you look grown up*
> *since childhood had barely been invented then*
> *or had been set aside for dark men*
> *much older than you;*
> *you probably wore short boots with buttons and a vest*
> *and shirtsleeves*
> *manufactured by unlucky little girls*
> *who weren't yet*
> *considered white.*

Through poetry, I speak directly to my great-grandfather, explaining why I write to him:

> *I need to write to speak to you*
> *because there's nowhere for my voice to go*
> *nothing for my voice to find now that you've*
> *lost your memory*
> *and gone to bed in the swamp, for good…*
> *I need to speak to you:*
> *it is urgent.*
> *I need to find you to make you innocuous.*
> *I need to bury you inside so that I can forgive you.*
> *I was seven years unborn when you died*
> *your body turning to sand*
> *and mine coming together…*

and uncovering him, letting him know that he's been found:

> *I can see you, walking down the aisle*
> *of Our Lady of Peace*
> *on that dirt road a short drive from the River,*

I can see you, severe in your Sunday suit
and shoes that betray your ambition
young doctor
kissing your virgin-white bride
on the eleventh of January, 1905…

and asking him questions that will never be answered:

…Was Hoover your man?
Did you drive a Packard?
Did you vote Democrat?
I can see you in the fall
of 1931
delivering babies, dangling them by the ankle
to make them breathe,
then cry…

Did you remember her?
Your child was wholesome, so wholesome
that she ripped the dates from all of her records
so that no one would know
the wounds of her birth.

Through poetry, I contemplate, too, ideas about race and whiteness when looking at my grandmother, who may have been reminded of the man who fathered her every time she looked at her own face:

…your blue-eyed girl
whom someone called an octoroon
so tragic
but she was so much whiter than that
white enough for even you to notice
but you never did…

and what, to me, is the bottom line:

July is the hottest month in this place
afternoon thunderstorms bring cool and wet for a little while
until the heat returns.
Did you hang mosquito netting over your bed?

> *Did you take her*
> *out in the woods*
> *or in your private practice*
> *or in a creaky old house that smelled of lye*
> *and generations of women's pain?*
> *Touse gave birth to a radiant little girl*
> *whom every man must have wanted*
> *except you.*

*

I don't want to see that man's face, my mother was told by her brother when she showed him the photograph that I found in the university archive. *That man was not her father.*

Unearthing my great-grandfather, whom I've called *Cornflower Blue* in other writings, triggered different responses in my family. Some of them had no interest in him and the details of his life (where is he buried?), but understandably continued the narrative that we'd always heard. Some of them expressed a distanced interest. I, as an historian and as a writer, focused keen attention not only on him, but on Touse, on Touse's parents and what certainly was a difficult time in their lives: their young daughter having the child of a white doctor, in a very small, rural, Catholic community. I pursued a long line of research on my ancestors who lived in the sugar parishes, trying to understand the family that Mema was born into, the heritage that she carried and that I, too, carry.

Many of my personal and historical essays shine light on my ancestresses, on my grandmother's grandmothers and their history as free women of color and mixed race women in Louisiana, as descendants of African enslaved people, of land-thieved Choctaw and Cherokee, of French, Spanish, German, and Irish men, as women who were oftentimes objectified because of their social status and their colonized beauty. I use the essay form to challenge, to unearth, to complicate, to interrogate, and ultimately, to venerate these women and their full lives beyond their phenotypes, beyond their external selves, beyond their condition as the objects of white men's desire. I use poetry, on the other hand, to converse with those who fathered the women in my family, those who, ironically, helped to define and delineate the lives of my ancestresses in the very act of leaving them fatherless. While I prefer to use the essay to excavate and decorate the lives of the women who came before me, to delve into their spiritual lives, to resuscitate the ways of love and worship and protection that they inherited from the women who came before them, poetry gives me the space to direct my thoughts to those who are seen as perpetrators and to expose them.

In history, men like my great-grandfather are culprits, lit by the spotlight of racial, socioeconomic, and gender privilege—and, indeed, they are. In poetry, they are listeners – a captive audience—receiving criticism, receiving forgiveness, receiving a focused, dynamic attention from those they never acknowledged. In poetry, I can say, *Whether you saw her or not, she was there. Whether you hear me or not, I will speak.*

Although my family lost Mema when I was just seventeen years old, her voice remains with me. Her facial expressions, her sense of humor, her fingers and fingernails, the way she hung onto me when we walked to the corner store, her laugh, her accent, the smells in her kitchen. Her name. Her house. Her history. All of it belongs to me on the cellular level, and it transforms into something linguistic. What begins in my own examination of my skin, my face, how much I look like my mother, my identity as a mixed race person who is the grandchild of four mixed race grandparents, ends in Mema's body, in her skin, in her love of me, in her unmatched existence as the woman who gave birth to the woman who gave birth to me, in her light-filled presence in the air, her movement in the winds that blow through the crepe myrtle and the cypress, her radiance in the waters that surround me, out here in New Orleans.

REFLECTIONS ON POETRY / REFLEXIONES SOBRE LA POESÍA

Ernesto L. Abeytia

Poetry is a mystical creature I'm still trying to figure out, *a long silent street where I walk in blackness and I stumble and fall*, as in Octavio Paz's "The Street." As an undergraduate, poetry was Shakespeare's sonnets, John Donne's flea with *our two bloods mingled*, Yeats's *coat covered with embroideries*, and John McCrae's *poppies blowing between the crosses, row on row*. During my M.A. in English, poetry became a mix of theory and criticism, Aristotle and Foucault, research methods dissecting the intercession of Plath and Bukowski. Now, nearing the end of my M.F.A., poetry is searching for myself, exploring my Spanish American heritage, reconciling *mi identidad de dos idiomas*, expressing myself in Spanish and English. And, for once in my academic career, I'm encountering works that speak to me as a bilingual writer and a bicultural person.

*

As the Bilingual Poet / *Como el poeta bilingüe*

When I was growing up, my parents primarily spoke English, only hinting at the Spanish world with words like *puerta* (door), *basura* (trash), or *mijo* (my son). They didn't use Spanish for anything other than simple, everyday nouns. For them, Spanish was understood, but never shared. For my grandparents, who raised me and with whom I lived as a child, Spanish was for whispering secrets between one another or for sharing laughter over coffee with friends.

For me, Spanish is a key to unlocking myself, a way of connecting to my history. Reading Julia Alvarez's poetry collection, *The Other Side/El Otro Lado*, I recognize that Spanish is political, a way of defining self and the surrounding world. In her poem "Bilingual Sestina," Alvarez writes, "Some things I have to say aren't getting said / in this snowy, blond, blue-eyed, gum-chewing English." I feel this sentiment acutely and explore it in my own poetry. Sometimes what I have to say doesn't fit the standard narrative or needs words as I know them, not as they're often prescribed. In much of my poetry, I blend Spanish and English because it's what's needed for the poem to work effectively. Though I learned Spanish primarily as an adult while living in Madrid, there are words and sentiments I first knew in Spanish and which don't have the same resonance for me in English. Some are really just vocabulary words learned once and then forgotten. But for me, these are the only words that make sense. Just as for Alvarez, "sol" means something more than just "sun," even the names and words used daily around us are more than they seem. I can't go into the Ventana Room at Arizona State University's Memorial Union without wondering at the lack of *ventanas* (windows) or think about the southeast corner's Rincon Room without laughing at the name *rincon* (corner). There is a world of words with clear, discernible meanings.

In one of my poems, I describe the experience of watching a bullfight, using common bullfighting terminology like *toreros* (bullfighters, generally), *matador* (star bullfighter), *banderilleros* (bullfighters who weaken the bull for the *matador*), and *palos* (decorated wooden sticks with barbed ends). These words have specific definitions not readily translatable or available in English. Including such words only available in Spanish is sometimes necessary for the poem. Yet, it's also sometimes dangerous since I risk isolating my readers with hyper-specificity or foreign terminologies and concepts. Working between two languages is difficult. Deciding which words to use and when/how to incorporate a foreign language can be tricky. My use of Spanish needs to always be deliberate, feel genuine. The last thing I want is to include Spanish superficially or superfluously.

More languages mean more ways of describing and more possibilities, but, as Alvarez suggests, sometimes those possibilities create confusion, offering even less clarity than before:

> ... *no English*
>
> *yet in my head to confuse me with translations, no English*
> *doubling the world with synonyms, no dizzying array of words*
> *—the world was simple and intact in Spanish—*
> luna, sol, casa, luz, flor, *as if the* nombres
> *were the outer skin of things, as if words were so close*
> *one left a mist of breath on things by saying*
>
> *their names, an intimacy I now yearn for in English ...*

Alvarez is right to want the intimacy of knowing. She has it in Spanish, wants it in

English. Perhaps this is what my parents tried to protect me from when they turned away from teaching me Spanish? They saw their parents' struggles to know the world fully in English, knew their own difficulties with assimilation, saw how language can "other," didn't want that for themselves or for their children. The result, though, is a conflict of self. I'm reclaiming the Spanish side of my identity through my writing because I feel disconnected. I want the intimacy Alvarez speaks of, and I want it in my writing across both languages. I want my poetry to work with and against Spanish and English to offer the parts of myself that can't be shared monolingually.

*

As the Traveling Poet / *Como el poeta viajero*

When I reflect on my current work and what I like to write about, I inevitably drift to thoughts of Spain, my brief life there, and my travels across it and its neighboring countries. There's something about the food, the people, the very air in Spain that pulls me to write about it. Beside my familial connections, I simply feel at home there, especially in Madrid, where I lived and studied for two years, and have gone back to visit many times since.

I first visited Spain in 2008, just after graduating from The University of Arizona. During this trip, I visited the capital city of Madrid, El Greco's Toledo, the aqueduct of Segovia, and the Monastery in El Escorial. I became so enamored with Spain that I returned for graduate school, attending Saint Louis University's Madrid campus. While there, I emerged myself in the city life that was so unlike Tucson, where I spent five years, or Phoenix, where I grew up, or even New York, where my father lived. Madrid, for me, was an enchantment—*me encanta!*—literally, it enchants me! Because Spain's *duende* continues to influence my writing, I'm drawn to poetry about Spain or poetry that has Spanish influences. Lee Anne Sittler is one such poet with a collection solely about Spain.

Lee Ann Sittler's collection *Extremadura* takes its name from her time living and writing in Extremadura, an autonomous community in the far west of Spain and bordering Portugal. *Extremadura*, Sittler's first book, is seductive, clever with language. Her poems weave together hope and despair, embroidering stories of life in Spain as both foreigner and native. The title piece, "Extremadura," is a long poem which opens and comprises roughly half the book. It begins by describing Extremadura and the emotions that resonate from living there:

> *You recognize, in its voice,*
> *your mother—*

something indistinguishable,
lost and trapped

between two hills. Someone
you never met

and have known your whole life,
all at once, and you meet her

for the first time in a foreign land,
in a non-native tongue,

thousands of miles away
from your last incarnation of home.

These opening lines speak of Extremadura in terms of an intimacy that goes beyond landscape. Rather, the poem is about more than a place—it's also about a feeling, a feeling of home and belonging. For Sittler, in whose mother's memory the book is written, the physical place comes to represent a surrogate mother who is both familiar yet foreign, embracing Sittler "in a non-native tongue, // thousands of miles away / from [her] last incarnation of home." This opening section informs the rest of the collection and its themes of belonging and longing while having lived in Spain for years, being fluent in the language, and yet still feeling like a foreigner.

In my own work, I find myself expressing similar sentiments of wanting to belong, while still feeling alien. Like Sittler, I am balancing between Spain as "foreign land" and "incarnation of home," my mispronounced sentiments marking me as *extranjero*. This struggle to know oneself is pertinent to my own writing as I use Spain to help inform my own identity. My surname is of Basque origin, yet I know very little of my family's history in the Basque Country or its traditions. My maternal surname is Castilian, which comes from central Spain and the country's former capital, Toledo. As I write about these places, I'm trying to uncover their pasts as much as my own. I want to understand myself in terms of Spanish history and how that history has shaped and continues to shape me.

*

As the Poet I Am / *Como el poeta yo soy*

Ultimately, I want my writing to be the best expression of myself that it can possibly be. I want it to be me as American, as Spanish, as husband, as brother, as son, as traveler, as storyteller, as bilingual, as bicultural, and as multifaceted. I choose what I read with the idea that these works help shape my writing, give me guidance, inspiration. I want poems and novels and short stories and everything I consume, to speak to me, challenge me, and, ultimately, make me better. I don't know if I'll do justice to them, but, I think, that's okay. Stories and poems aren't meant to be read once or twice and move on from. They're meant to be loved and admired and continuously sought and returned to. They represent the best of us. They also represent the best to which I aspire. I know that if I continue to write with great work in mind and with great works as guides, I'll produce the work I want to produce, the work that is me at my best.

DESTROYED OUT OF HER THE GREAT VOICE: ON WRITING AS A DISABLED FILIPINA AMERICAN POET

Abigail Licad

Around the time of my most acute manic episode that led me to swallow a bottle of sleeping pills, I started to write poetry. Although a decade has now passed, I still can't bring myself to read through the desperate scrawl that fills my old notebooks. I've tried twice, but each time I would begin to feel the symptoms of an anxiety attack: troubled breathing, racing thoughts, sweaty palms, an overwhelming fear that the oncoming attack will be the one to do me in.

I've failed at all my attempts through poetry or prose to adequately describe my firsthand experiences of mania. Even the most thoughtful and intricate metaphors are inadequate. The best I can say is that when I was right in the center of a full-blown hypomanic attack, I just wanted all the excessiveness to end. Mostly, I pleaded for my racing thoughts to stop. They kept me awake for nights in a row and left me physically exhausted.

To any "normal" mind, my thoughts followed no logic. But to me, my thoughts aggregated into grandiose truths. My brand of lunacy may have fallen short of hallucinations or hearing voices, but I believed that I could read minds. I thought I could decipher the motivations of all family members and friends. I believed they were all plotting a hateful conspiracy against me. I was unable to feel love—not from others, not for others, and especially, not for myself.

As the rapid-cycling, polyphonic thoughts in my head multiplied, I felt compelled to write as many of them down as possible. It was a way to purge some and make room for all the other new thoughts that kept frantically sprouting in my mind. Since I considered my thoughts to be nothing short of revelations, I concluded that verse was the only fitting expression for them. The "poems" I wrote were quite bad. I was no Romantic visionary genius like Blake or Wordsworth. I did not have the capacity to edit in any disciplined way. All I produced were clamorous ramblings of a severely crippled, disjointed mind. Still, I thought of each line as a poetic unit, each one aiming, however feebly and desperately, at deeper truths.

While writing helped me exorcise thoughts, reading poetry helped me to slow them down. I didn't read for coherence across stanzas. Rather, I read for just *any* shred of understanding. Comprehending even just one portion of a poem—an image, a brief observation, a musical phrase—was catalyst enough for my over-sensitized, over-stimulated brain to derive endless layers of meaning. I may not have been able to synthesize aspects of a poem to form a holistic interpretation, but somehow, I felt able to access its core emotions, to feel them so intensely that my moods grew elated or depressed in reaction. I hung onto every word for dear life. In this way, poetry saved me.

Or at the very least, poetry gave me a way to cope. It gave me a way to redirect all the internal noises that were wearing me out. In choosing to immerse myself in poetry, I asserted my will. Poetry led me to choose existence over nothingness, thereby keeping me from seeking ultimate silence and final reprieve.

Utterly Broken

I was 28 years old when I was finally diagnosed with Bipolar II Disorder. I had been experiencing episodes of undiagnosed depression perhaps as early as high school, but it was the virulent, cyclical mania that finally brought me to a doctor. I was immediately put under powerful antipsychotic drugs that left me sleepy and lethargic for most of the time. It would take another six years before a doctor found the most effective medication and dosages to rid me of a larger part of my cycling moods. I am currently on six different daily medications, but dark moods still sometimes descend upon me suddenly, often without reason.

For a long time, I wrestled with deep shame over my diagnosis. Although I could understand from an abstract standpoint that the debilitating extremes of melancholia and rage materialized through no fault of my own, I hated myself for being a failure. I was no better, I thought, than the literary and psychoanalytic stereotypes of the insane woman proffered by the patriarchal, Eurocentric education that I had been working so hard to disprove through my accomplishments. Because there was no "trigger" to my malady, I had to be somehow genetically predisposed. But rather than excusing my culpability, my "natural," hereditary instability seemed to me to agree with the gendered notions of sickness that continue to inform society's beliefs and representations of the mentally ill: women, being a weaker mental and physical embodiment compared to men, were far more susceptible to hysteria and derangement. In other words, I failed to overcome the weakness expected of my sex.

Since my focus in this essay is to trace the relationship between my personal need to write poetry and my illness, I need not dive into a historical overview of Western discourses on mania and madness. The misogynistic, patriarchal notions that still inform the lexicon of mental illness today—from Aristotle's view of women as "monstrosities" in *Generation of Animals* to Freud's attribution of "neuroses" to women in *The Interpretation of Dreams*—exceed the scope of this essay.

It's enough for now to say that the cultural and intellectual inheritance of these constructions provides a shortcut for people to "read" me and form conclusions. Because I am a woman, any sign of imbalance or disruption erases the distinctiveness of my experiences. It's all too easy to classify me among the other "madwomen in the attic," to pathologize all of my actions and speech as symptomatic of my illness, to erase my agency in how I choose to represent myself.

Despite my awareness of the social construction of my ailment, the stigmatization of mania as some sort of deviant and contagious phenomenon prevailed in my mind as I started seeing myself through the lens of ignorant opinions. I felt expelled from the patriarchal expectations of female beauty and desirability. I felt freakish, deformed, inherently inferior, and damaged. I existed in a spectrum at the opposite end of "the ideal." These thoughts led to psychic self-flagellation. "Who will love me now?" I often asked myself. My chances of attaining the conventional trappings of a full, successful life—marriage, children, economic stability, happiness—felt thoroughly quashed. I mourned the many impossibilities leveled upon me by my disorder.

Convinced by others' reproaches that I needed to "pull myself together"—for my affliction was "all in the mind"—I searched for acceptable causes for what ailed me. I had no "real" reason for going crazy. Unlike the frenzied Sisa in Jose Rizal's *Noli Me Tangere* roaming the streets calling the names of her dead sons who were murdered by Spanish colonizers, or Shakespeare's Lady Macbeth who kills herself due to unbearable guilt from orchestrating a murder, I have not suffered from any trauma caused by war or rape, or any other tragedy.

However, the growing number of psychiatric studies on people of color may provide a partial explanation. These studies hypothesize that the higher proportion of depression and manic-depressive diagnoses among people of color is due to the additional stressors brought on by race- and class-related struggles. Such struggles are compounded in the case of women. Certainly, my personal experiences confirm this hypothesis. In my case, the intense pressure to live up to the "model minority" myth as an Asian American might have led to the deterioration of my health.

At the height of my most manic episode, I was in the midst of deciding on my next step toward achieving model minority status. I had just returned to the San Francisco Bay Area after three years abroad—two in England where I graduated with an MPhil in literature from Oxford University, and one in Senegal where I worked as a volunteer for a health organization that educated rural communities against the practice of female genital cutting. My life was in flux as I tried to reintegrate into American culture. Uncertain over my values and who I truly was, or perhaps afraid that my true calling did not conform to conventional definitions of success, I let the expectations of the model minority myth dictate my goals. Rather than pursue my burgeoning interests in poetry and writing, I prepared to take the law school entrance exam while working as a paralegal at a top Silicon Valley law firm.

Because I had grown up in the Philippines until I was 13 and struggled with third-world poverty firsthand, the pressure to become an immigrant success story weighed heavily upon me. Economic success, and the social respect and admiration it brings, would not only demonstrate gratitude for my parents' sacrifices, but would also redeem them from their diminished status as part of a "silent" immigrant class in America. Despite their college degrees and strong work ethic, my parents had to resign themselves to debased job opportunities offered by an American capitalistic system that devalued immigrants of color.

I may be wrong, but at times it seems to me that the pressure I felt, which manifested in an unforgiving drive to succeed, was exacerbated by being a first-generation immigrant. Unlike second-generation Asian Americans who perhaps inherit more diluted forms of pressure from their immigrant parents, the ambition that drove me originated first and foremost within myself. From the moment I stepped off the plane in America, I decided to impose upon myself the responsibility of raising my family's social status.

My mostly white psychotherapists found it difficult to understand my extreme fear of failing at my ambitions when "failing" for me, at the time, meant anything less than achieving the best. Despite all my therapists' encouragement, I resisted the definition of happiness as self-fulfillment because it seemed entirely alien and even selfish to me as an immigrant. It was so contrary to the most rhetorical of immigrant questions: "Why choose to earn less money when you have the choice to earn more?" In other words, why choose a "frivolous," impractical vocation as a writer that risked material comfort, especially when you grew up poor?

As I failed to reach the ambitions that would gain me acceptance into the dominant class, I experienced my first nervous breakdown. I began to rapidly cycle between the darkest depression and most acute, uncontrollable mania.

The Wounded Shall Groan

No friend or family member has ever asked me directly what it's like to have bipolar disorder. Each time I've revealed my illness to someone, I am met with a curious look, and then, silence. Not the silence of understanding or quiet sympathy, but a silence, it seems to me, of refusal. In their desire to switch topics, to elide the confession that had just occurred, to pretend that nothing significant has happened and quickly resume normal conversation, I sense their discomfort. Perhaps they would rather not know, perhaps the intimacy is unbearable. Or perhaps they don't ask questions because sensationalized stereotypes and clichés from mainstream media populate their silence—they presume to already know about mental illness, and it scares them.

Despite the efforts of my mother's family to guard their tragic stories in secrecy, as a child I heard whispers from cousins about an uncle who shot himself alone in his room, an aunt whose stomach had to be pumped after a drug overdose, an elder cousin who had to be institutionalized for reacting violently to voices in his head. It became clear to me after my own diagnosis that depression and schizophrenia ran in my blood. I felt angry that such knowledge had been shrouded in shameful secrecy. Had I been informed of this history of mental illness in my family, I would likely have sought help sooner, and been diagnosed and treated sooner. And, however futile it may be of me to suppose, I might have achieved more success in life, rather than blaming myself for wasting the many golden opportunities that had been presented to me.

Because conspicuous physical "markers" of disability like wheelchairs or hearing aids are not employed by those who live with mental illness, we are often handled with suspicion and disbelief. To this day, my parents still deny my chronic illness, as though doing so would banish it. They refuse to believe that my last manic episode is symptomatic of a permanent condition that I've inherited. While visiting me just a few days ago, my mother expressed surprise and confusion upon seeing medicine bottles on my nightstand—why wasn't I cured yet, she asked.

The culture of illness in our society worships the "cure" as its god, which equates to an inability to accept chronic illness and disability. As a result, disability is seen as ruining a person's life. It is seen as the most intolerable of states to inhabit. Many who suffer from depression or bipolar disorder refuse to self-identify as "disabled" in an effort to empower themselves, as though accepting the label would be akin to accepting defeat and owning a sort of inferiority. They fail to realize that more progress and legal mechanisms could be put in place for accommodating those with disabilities if only we, as a society, would stop idealizing the "abled" and accept that disability is a state that defines each of us in some way, at least eventually in old age.

The widespread inability to accept and accommodate disability makes it all the more important for me to affirm here, publicly and for the first time, in my own "coming-out" narrative, that I have bipolar disorder. For me, claiming my mental illness and the label of being a disabled Filipina American woman writer, is a political act. Slowly, I am trying to feel more comfortable with no longer hiding the truth in shame. If I am to live honestly, with integrity, and believe in my own self-love and acceptance, then I must be comfortable not only with others' discovery of my illness but also with my own declaration of it – unapologetically and without shame.

For me, starting to speak through writing and poetry began even before it was a conscious decision. I started slowly, first by venturing out of the white, literary canon into which I had been submerged and reading Filipino American authors. Shortly after I started feeling more coherent from medication, I stumbled upon Eileen Tabios' poetry book review blog *Galatea Resurrects*. Since Tabios published nearly all of the poetry reviews she received, I was able to muster the courage to submit.

For my first book review, I chose *Pinoy Poetics*, the anthology of Filipino and Filipino American essays and poems edited by Nick Carbó. I can still vividly recall details from the day I received my review copy in the mail. I remember running to my father with the book, proudly showing him the front illustration of a young brown man sitting atop a parcel wrapped in an American flag. It was for me one of the most joyous experiences of my self-education—here finally was proof of a literary inheritance that shared in the same history and experiences as my own. The introduction alone presented a key revelation—the first of many to come. At one point, Carbó observes that "When one sees himself/herself in a respected work of literature, it is a powerful and validating moment." And indeed, there I was, hunched over the book on my desk, drugged up on a cocktail of downers and the magic pill that is Abilify, my frantic mood swings beginning at last to settle, finally experiencing the moment of validation that would lead me to find a voice with which to speak.

When Her Waves Do Roar Like Great Waters

I may have at last found forebears who speak of immigrant and racial experiences similar to my own, yet I have still to find mentors in the form of authors who also identify as disabled writers. The recent emergence of the bipolar memoir as a genre has exposed me to many writers who explore mental illness, but an overwhelming number of them are middle- to upper-class white women. Despite my vigilant efforts, I have yet to discover a Filipino or Asian American who writes about the experiences of a manic-depressive life.

In the bipolar memoirs I have read, a consistent storyline prevails. The speaker traces her life's trajectory from "normalcy" to extreme mania (involving hallucinations, dangerously distorted judgment, sex and shopping sprees, etc.), to a sudden, frightful descent into the darkest depression, and then finally, to healing. Although my experiences have been similar, my own story diverges in its lack of a "happy ending."

Despite suffering the maniacal ravages of bipolar symptoms and suicide attempts much worse than mine, all of the writers I've read have managed to eventually succeed in elite jobs as doctors, lawyers, or professors. I used to feel much guilt after reading these memoirs—why haven't I been able to make "more" of myself than the menial admin-heavy work that paid my bills. On the one hand, it did occur to me that these women's positions of privilege permitted them better access to well-connected and stronger support networks and more expensive healthcare, whereas the average woman of color has less access to proper treatment, let alone to leisure time for writing a memoir. On the other hand, I also took into consideration that my own illness was not as extreme or debilitating as theirs—as if the experience of illness could somehow be measured hierarchically.

Although I am surviving and living a relatively "healthy" life, I feel that, unlike these memoirists who have arrived at glamorously successful and triumphant conclusions, an incipient imbalance is constantly simmering in my blood, threatening to sweep me away into full-blown manic or depressive episodes at a random moment's notice. I am always aware that I am only one small step away from losing my job, and just one lost paycheck away from poverty. My illness looms as an ever-present threat, waiting to take away everything I have.

However, my sense of an absent happy ending in my life story thus far has, I believe, proven to be a benefit to my writing process. At this point, poetry has been a vehicle for me to parse out a feeling, thought, hunch, or memory. I consider myself to be an "aspiring" poet because most of my poems don't seem to reach beyond the meditative. I have yet to acquire versatility in my use or experimentation with language, for instance. I suspect that being self-identified as a disabled woman of color has been key to my inability to arrive at resolution in my writing. I find that I must continue to unpack, parse out, and explore, or else I become complicit in the social and cultural structures that place me at a greater risk for poor mental health to begin with. Always in my poems my meditations circle through the triple axes of race, class, and gender, and loop in further notions of otherness, diaspora, history, and the postcolonial.

Because the Spoiler Is Come on Her

It has taken me months to write this essay. Despite the considerable progress I have made in finally "owning" my illness and the courage it has taken me to slowly reveal my bipolar disorder to friends and relatives one by one, making the knowledge public to strangers whose reactions are fully out of my control as I am doing here right now causes me a new kind of anxiety. Not the anxiety of an oncoming panic attack emanating from chemical imbalances within, but the kind of anxiety a soldier about to go into battle would have in facing external attackers.

Foremost among my worries are the opportunities that might be denied to me due to knowledge about my illness. A potential friend, partner, employer, mentor, or ally might cursorily reject me upon their discovery of my bipolar disorder rather than challenge themselves to understand, let alone read this essay in its entirety. The whispers might spread. The judgments might rain.

Perhaps my only unselfish worry is the shame that my family might feel from the revelation I am now making to the world. They might believe that my illness reflects upon them in some way. That they are always implicated in every hostile, fearful, suspicious, dismissive opinion levied upon me. Should my parents confront me about breaking the silence they themselves have practiced, I already have my response prepared: *It's not my fault. It's not your fault, either. But it is your fault that I'm not a coward.*

As I wrote this essay, I did not know whether I would submit it at the end. If I didn't, then the energy it took to write it would still be useful psychic and emotional experience nonetheless. If I did submit, I told myself I would likely realize a new freedom, but hopefully not at the cost of ignorant persecutions. Whatever comes, I will at least feel consoled by the fact that my illness is what led me to finally discover my true calling as a poet. Perhaps in time I will feel an even greater feeling than being consoled—perhaps I will even be grateful.

DESPERATE & BEAUTIFUL NOISE

Tim Seibles

> *…Well, I stand up next to a mountain*
> *chop it down with the edge of my hand*
> *Well, I pick up all the pieces and make an island*
> *Might even raise a little sand.*
>
> —Jimi Hendrix

As I enter what must be the last third of my life and realize I've given half my waking hours to writing poems, I can't help but think about Jimi Hendrix—that guitar god of The Sixties—known to practice obsessively 12-14 hours a day and, not so rarely, forgetting to eat. Why did he do it? Why do any of us try so hard to bend the silence, to fashion a voice worthy of a listen?

James Marshall Hendrix, born in 1943, grew up in Seattle. According to his aunt, he was an odd child, shy and often "sitting alone, thinking like a little old man." Who knew, then, that inside this boy, who sometimes used cardboard to cover gaps in the soles of his shoes, resided the seed of a voice that would change the way electric guitar would be played for a long time—and perhaps forever. What made him take on the given world with his desperate and beautiful noise?

Surely, the sociopolitical circumstances of the time were heavily fortified against him: his mother's early death, his father's reluctance to spend "good money" on a guitar, and rock music itself was almost entirely the dominion of white musicians. Black people were *supposed* to think R&B and dream of Motown.

Of course, there are those who have said (and will say) that it was this rough crucible that made him, that fertilized his potential. I can only point to the millions of people born and raised with such privation and ask about their general and often misery-laden silence. Others will toss out the catchall word "genius," which I find painfully empty as an explanation, unless we consider genius a kind of high octane fuel for manic effort.

I am both mystified and inspired by the fact that Hendrix, in spite of so much, brought to light a sound that made an indelible mark on the Sixties, the era during which the foundation of my faith in life was built. I still find his music central to my soul, though I've been listening to it since I was twelve, when my older brother put *Electric Ladyland* on our mom's old record player and turned it up.

What do I hear when that guitar is playing? Rage? Love? A stand against a world ravaged by bad ideas? The "dark sounds" of Lorca's *duende*? Whatever I hear, I'm pretty sure it's *not* exactly what he heard. Like all hard-earned artistic expression, his music is both a foray into the cultural discourse and an intimate but incomplete look at the otherwise indecipherable subconscious life of a person. Nonetheless, I am carried by that sound to destinations unreachable by other means. (Is there any place like "Voodoo Chile"?) It strikes me, that no matter what he was after, I needed that voice, that lacerating and tender attack on the silence—and this makes me think about *voice* in all its forms.

At first glance, the development of a guitarist's voice may seem unrelated to a poet's, but syntax does imply a kind of linguistic melody—and when we consider ascending and descending inflections, assonance and consonance, the turning (or phrasing) of lines, rhythm, rhyme, tone, and the way both music and verse move through time, the relationship between instrumental and poetic utterance becomes evident. Though words have specific definitions and musical notes do not, both *do* mean—unless we are to believe that what is expressed through harmony and melody is not food for emotionally charged reflection, which seems clearly false.

> *…What's madness but nobility of soul*
> *At odds with circumstance? The day's on fire!*
> *I know the purity of pure despair,*
> *My shadow pinned against a sweating wall.*
> *That place among the rocks—is it a cave,*
> *Or winding path? The edge is what I have.*
>
> *A steady storm of correspondences!*
> *A night flowing with birds, a ragged moon,*
> *and in broad day the midnight come again!*
> *A man goes far to find out what he is—*
> *Death of the self in a long tearless night,*
> *All natural shapes blazing unnatural light.*
>
> *Dark, dark my light, and darker my desire.*
> *My soul, like some heat-maddened summer fly,*

Keeps buzzing at the sill. Which I is I?
A fallen man, I climb out of my fear.
The mind enters itself and God the mind
and one is One, free in the tearing wind.

– Theodore Roethke, from "In A Dark Time"

When we think about voice, generally, we think of an individual speaking (writing) from a single position—his heart, her mind—but it is worth considering that a voice can be representative or *stand-in* for a community's voice. And, though one might rightly think of community in narrow terms—race, gender, class, or sexual identity—the idea of community also cuts across such boundaries to include members of many different groups who share a sensibility, a particular *feeling* about life. ("Hendrix Freaks" came in many colors and from many nations.)

We often think of "crossover" artists as musicians but, of course, there are crossover poets as well who capture perspectives, sensations—felt understandings—that wide varieties of people embrace. June Jordan, Amiri Baraka, Ai, and Pablo Neruda, come readily to mind.

In the broadest sense, a time, a place, a *culture* is a crucible from which ideas, actions, and voices emerge. If I am a black singer, for example, my heart will likely have been forged by circumstances specific to my experience, but what I sing may reach people of many backgrounds because we share the entire spectrum of emotion. (Black grief and White grief overlap quite a bit, I think—as do gay and straight glee.) This is why a straight Latina might feel a passionate connection to the music of Tracy Chapman and why a Black kid who grew up in a gang-ridden part of Philadelphia might become an adult who loves Theodore Roethke's poems.

What we want from the guitar, the piano, the sax, the cello is similar to what we crave in a poem—which is a kind of vocal solo. In our daily lives, we are submerged in half-light, surrounded by stolid faces: people who express themselves partly or who use language calculated precisely to mislead. Even in intimacy, much that is said is rooted in a sense of obligation, a sense of what is *supposed* to be said. (I love you: now you say it back…*or else.*)

What we love about good music is exactly what we love about good poetry: the absence of trickery, the presence of honesty: every word intended to enliven, to enlighten, to carry what is *sayable* to the full extent that language allows. Stephen Dunn calls this "crucial speech" and believes it to be an antidote to the barely disguised horseshit that spews from the mouths of many politicians, preachers, and TV talking heads—whether they're selling bigger burgers or casting the news.

> *I will die in Paris, on a rainy day,*
> *on some day I can already remember.*
> *I will die in Paris—and I don't step aside—*
> *perhaps on a Thursday as today is Thursday, in autumn.*
>
> *It will be a Thursday because today, Thursday, setting down*
> *these lines, I have put my upper arm bones on*
> *wrong, and never so much as today have I found myself,*
> *With all the road ahead of me, alone…*

– Cesar Vallejo, from "Black Stone Lying on a White Stone"

What brings me back to the music of Jimi Hendrix again and again is the same thing that has me reading and re-reading Robert Hayden, Lucille Clifton, Basho, Anne Sexton. In the presence of such work, I am convinced that everything—the sounds, the silence, every word, every *note*—is there for the sole purpose of communicating the essential thing.

I believe there is a profound and pervasive hunger for such authenticity. I would go so far as to say that *cynicism*, a kind of cancer of the spirit, begins with the nagging suspicion that most human action has its roots in deceit. Too often, we secretly hold the hearts of our fellow citizens in contempt. Some may even hold their own hearts in contempt. This makes empathy impossible. Compassion seems naïve, impractical—which makes genuine community the first casualty. (This is why movements like *Black Lives Matter* come to be.)

Nobody, who is sane, wants to live without faith in other people, without faith in the world to which we are born. That treading such anguish is a common state of mind makes evident the tragic failings of the societies that have developed. Nobody *really* wants to wait till the afterlife for fulfillment. The prevailing interest in ideologies—religious or secular—that perceive human life as a problem to *transcend* or *fix* through fascist intimidation is based upon a type of projected self-loathing, another by-product of cynicism.

It strikes me that those who spend their lives trying to talk back to this world are, in many cases, offering a corrective—a different sense of things that correlates more readily with the fundamental imperatives of human association: emotional frankness, attentiveness to what is felt, a sharp turn toward the knowledge that all of us are equally lonely, equally vulnerable to the damage that cruelty and greed inflict. What is authenticity but an affront to all that is *in*authentic, a way to break through all that is at odds with what we *know* in our bones?

> ...*but when i wake to the heat of morning*
> *galloping down the highway of my life*
> *something hopeful rises in me*
> *rises and runs me out into the road*
> *and i lob my fierce thigh high*
> *over the rump of the day and honey*
> *i ride i ride*
>
> – Lucille Clifton, from "Hag Riding"

A poem, a song, a guitar solo: any form of human expression that takes seriously the project of opening the heart is subversive to the exact extent that the surrounding culture denies the primacy and abiding complexity of our emotions. This is partly why artists are often viewed as "weird," why arts funding is often scarce in our schools but it seems there's always money for football. Why is *toughness*, the will to ignore or hide what is felt, such a celebrated feature of masculinity (and adulthood in general)?

There is no *neutral* living. Either our actions significantly reflect our felt sense of things or we perform our lives *in spite of* what we feel. We live against the grain of our authenticity—which is, at its core, a formula for chronic frustration, depression, perhaps violence and complete madness. (What's behind the opioid epidemic? The fetishizing of guns? The militarization of the police?—and the rise of *Trumpism*, here and around the globe?)

Why did so many bands of the Sixties start playing so loud? In its most humane forms, the fundamental urge to say begins when we realize that what we hear inside ourselves has no true correlative in the society to which we belong. If a person found the external world in harmony with her inner world there would be little need to begin the arduous and terribly lonely task of shaping a distinct voice in an effort to assert a truth where previously a void *or* something contrary to the heart held sway.

I believe that it is this urge, this hunger to put into words what seems to have been forgotten or missed or intentionally silenced, that continues to drive my compulsion to figure out what I mean and write it down. This might be the energizing principal for *anyone* who invents a new way to engage the world we share. Perhaps the critical thing we learn from the artists we love—be they guitarists or poets (painters or dancers)—is to trust and value that itch inside our guts, that restlessness that means something we know has got to get *said*.

MY LIFE IS NOT A STEREOTYPE THOUGH SOMETIMES WRITING ABOUT IT FEELS THAT WAY OR *HABLANDO POR UN TUBO Y SIETE LLAVES*

Melissa Coss Aquino

Oye me, when writing from conditions and communities that feel under siege, untangling the story you need to tell from the one people want to hear is the work of lifetimes, and yet, sometimes, when you are writing to survive because it has become the place you go, and the thing you do, to drag the net through the river to keep your drinking water clean, it becomes increasingly more difficult to do. Moving past the poetics of survival, if that can even be done, is a tangled tango of competing wants and needs. The task of untangling has to be placed like a bull's eye target just above whatever corner of the world you have carved out for writing, and you need to stare it down and figure it out, with precision; you must learn how to control the bow and unleash that arrow, not for your readers, though you hope, but for yourself because you must. Your survival really does depend on it. Those who argue it doesn't don't know suicide, addiction and self-annihilation. But you do, so you keep pulling your net through the river. You keep pulling on the tension of your bow and releasing arrows. One by one.

For so many of us that target we are aiming for is the tiny space where we manage to tell the truth without enacting stereotypes long used against us, but sometimes our truth feels like a long list of stereotypes no matter which way we turn. I stare at the bull's eye of my own vision, work against the compelling, sometimes irresistible, desire to look over my shoulder and wonder who is watching and what they might think, and keep trying to hit the truth. One arrow at a time. Each bull's eye a moving target. Esa habla por un tubo y siete llaves as my grandmother likes to say when insulting the wordy ones who like to tell truths out loud, who talk too much and about a lot of nothing. It is supposed to be an insult, but it means talking from one true source even if it is coming out from various spigots and faucets all at the same time. Talking too much and all at once. Talking and talking until you finally say what you mean. Talking until someone finally listens. Replace talking with writing. Replace too much with never enough. Some will label it: wasteful, annoying, and repetitive. You must anoint it: required. If you are looking to find the thing you are actually trying to say, you better open all those faucets until you hit the one spilling clean water and clearest truth. My arrival at the writing life has been about learning, that unlike water, words don't require our careful conservation, especially when they have been denied free range, free flow, for centuries. Open the faucets. Do it. Teach it. Bear witness and read it. This is not only about selling books or winning prizes, though we will also do that. This is about cleaning the waters of our creative lives stream by stream, roomful by roomful, in communities of two or two hundred. I have chosen to examine the seven llaves, the faucets through which my truth sometimes spills, but the word llaves in Spanish also means keys, like the keys to rooms in Bluebeard's castle. Remember that the one marked with blood, that you're expressly forbidden from using, is also the one that will save your life if you have the courage to face reality and open that door.

Llave #1

Pick, at random, almost any of the maddening statistics/stereotypes/half-truths/blatant lies about: my community, The Bronx, my people, Puerto Ricans from the Bronx, or myself, a Puerto Rican woman born and raised in the Bronx. Poverty. Welfare. Drug addiction. Alcoholism. Drug dealing. Teen parents. Parental abandonment. Poor health outcomes for preventable and treatable diseases. We could go on, but let's not. There are lots of studies done on all the ways in which we don't function. Lots of statistics to tell you all the ways we fail to thrive. It is a sub-genre of the *NY Times* since the 1950's when there was declared a literal situation referred to as "the Puerto Rican Problem" because we had arrived in huge numbers (some years 40,000 at a time) and we arrived with American citizenship we never asked for, but quickly began to use to register to vote. We arrived with tongues wrapped in Spanish and love into schools and jobs that worked hard to beat it out of us. We posed our biggest "problem" by being racially unfit for a country so clearly set on black and white; we had the audacity to arrive in every shade of black, white, brown and beige, married and commingled. It was the fifties. People forget that our arrival must have felt and looked like a nightmare come true to all those trying to secure the American future from such freedom. We were treated accordingly. Here, in the refusal to fit but longing to survive, is born a poetics of discontent through which we are read, and then must read ourselves. Did you pick one of the entrenched dysfunctions from the limited list above? Any one of the ones listed, and several that are not, can be applied directly to my life, and not by extended family (though there is plenty there too), but right in the tight concentric circle of a tiny group of people to which I belong, and from whom I emerged, and who I love deeply though not without complications.

This statistical information makes for controversial subject matter everywhere I go.

Ay mija esa' cosa no se hablan. Por Dios. The story has become a thing I can't tell without pissing someone off or carving a new wound where an old wound had just been trying to heal. Our poetics, built upon a rock of trying to prove our worthiness, is constantly crashing like water up against a damn trying to hold it back, re-route it, and tell it how to flow and where to go so that others might know us better, like us better. Hate us less? But how would we sound if we were only trying to know ourselves? Each other?

Llave #2

So let's begin this story another way. Let's try to tell it the way some people would like it told. I am an Assistant Professor of English at Bronx Community College. I have an MFA and am currently writing my dissertation for a PhD in English from the CUNY Graduate Center. I just signed my first book contract with The Center for Puerto Rican Studies. Both of my sons are beautiful creative spirits and good men. One in college, one a recent graduate of City College. I have been happily married for twenty-five years to a Dominican man who arrived at twenty-two and spoke no English and is the embodiment of the American Dream, in terms of his achievements. He is also a loving father and fierce and gentle warrior committed to justice, truth and light. He is completing a PhD at the CUNY Graduate Center in Political Science. We bought a house in the Bronx in a complicated space between Riverdale and Lehman College that is undergoing its own transformations from working class to gentrified, but there is still an empty lot on our block and a community center across the street, in addition to Starbucks, Target and TJ Maxx within walking distance. Our home, like our lives, exists at a cross current of possibilities and futures embedded in deeply laid grooves of the past. This is, after all, the way I am supposed to tell the story. The official version I am supposed to use to tell everyone "we are not like you think we are." I am supposed to tell it as some kind of "pull yourself up by the bootstraps" story of hard work and achievement always being linked. I am supposed to tell it with pride and hide the rest in shame. Except that is not a story. That is public relations. Art is not public relations. As one of my intellectual and spiritual mothers, Audre Lorde, wrote in her magical essay "Poetry is Not A Luxury," "The quality of light by which we scrutinize our lives has direct bearing upon the product which we live, and upon the changes which we hope to bring about through those lives. It is within this light that we form those ideas by which we pursue our magic and make it realized." This essay is required reading in my Intro to Creative Writing course. Stay in that space with me one second before we move on. What magic can we pursue, and what quality of light can we use to scrutinize our lives, if we can't say out loud what really happened to us, what is still happening to us? How will we make that magic realized?

Llave #3

OK so let's try again. As a writer, and an academic, I have been in rooms too numerous to count from undergrad all the way to a few weeks ago (a span of more than twenty-eight years) where some version of this kind of conversation plays out:

"Oh great more work about Puerto Rican drug addicts, that is the last thing we need."

"Why do we (you) keep performing the same stereotypes white people have perpetrated against us for all these years?"

"Why is it that only books and movies about our criminality and poverty sell?"

"Wasn't all that shit in the past. Look at you now. Write about that. That's what we need to be promoting." (Note the public relations slant as if art is supposed to promote as opposed to reveal and allow and heal and hold)

"People who write about those things are just looking for attention and pity. Poor me stories."

" … and right away they want to make the college student someone struggling to cut ties with his life on the streets. We are not all gang members."

Except some of us are or were or might have been if not for the teacher, the guidance counselor, the cousin or the aunt, the one that stepped in between you and the abyss. We could go on, but let's not. This is enough to make the point. It is always another Latino/a imposing a kind of silencing that I am accustomed to in a world that could care less about The Bronx, the poor, or the "Puerto Rican Problem", but that never fails to wound deeply, even after twenty-eight years, because it ends in someone I consider "safe" calling me, my life, and my uncanny resemblance to so many statistics, even in my defiance of them, a stereotype. "Don't talk about that crap because it makes us look bad, it's so over-done, because what we really need is Jane the Virgin or Lin Manuel Miranda. Look at Hamilton! Now that is creativity!"

Yes, yes it is creative, and wonderful, and I am proud of every single instance of Latino/a creative and intellectual accomplishment even if it doesn't speak to me or my experience because I don't believe there is a single story for any group. Chimamanda Ngozi Adichie brilliantly captures this in "The Danger of a Single Story" and even found herself in a single-story mind trap around transgender women she couldn't quite escape. We are all trying to figure out, for we are not born knowing, how to speak bravely and freely our own truth with the responsibility to represent a people, long maligned, on our backs. Alice Walker beautifully captured this complex space of how we tell who we are and who we love, and still get burned, in a book she wrote entirely dedicated to working through the negative response she received from the African American community to *The Color Purple*. Walker wrote/curated a collection of letters, articles, journal entries, photographs and writing meant to capture the communal in all its complexity in the book, *The Same River Twice, Honoring the Difficult*, to work through the pain of feeling utterly misunderstood by "her people." First, when the book *The Color Purple* was released and then again when the movie was directed by Steven Spielberg. The preface is only two pages, but should be given as a meditation tool for all writers of color to begin to distinguish the mirrors we need from the mirrors we seek. Walker writes, "I belong to a people so wounded by betrayal, so hurt by misplacing their trust…I belong to a people, heart and mind, who do not trust mirrors. Not those, in any case, in which we ourselves appear…Art is the mirror, perhaps the only one, in which we can see our true collective face. We must honor its sacred function. We must let art help us."

Walker is writing about the ways some people long degraded want to use art to show only what they feel has not been shown that reflects our light, our qualities, our best selves. She is also making clear that this is not the function of art. I am all about my best self, but I am also keenly aware that not everyone where I come from has had the opportunity to even learn that concept. That does not make the selves they became something to hide or be ashamed of or used to define who we are, or are not, as a people. And I, despite all the public relations worthy material in my adult life résumé, am still the daughter of two people ravaged by drug addiction, and a family decimated by poverty and all of its complications and illnesses. We are also still a family bound in love, and we are, most of us, still alive. As June Jordan wrote, "We Did Not All Die." The one cannot be held exclusive from the other, nor are they a correlated proof of something special about me. This is a challenge to create a poetics of truth that must sustain, in the inimitable Gloria Anzaldúa's term, a "borderland identity"— a migrant's path of crossing borders and languages without demanding proof of status. I am exactly who I say I am, who I write I am, even as I am also that which cannot be written. Even if what I write doesn't make you feel good about yourself.

Llave #4

Que diran la gente. Eso no se habla. Ay que verguenza. My first published essay was a tiny little thing called "Una Sinverguenza" in *Callaloo*, submitted under the loving guidance of Emily Raboteau, while I was in my MFA program at City College. I would have never submitted it for publication were it not for her, and in some ways it was both horrifying and liberating to have it all out, all at once. All siete llaves pouring out the truth. Though it was buried in so much silence and subterfuge you could barely hear it, that essay was the sound of me crawling out of a shame bred so deep into me I barely knew who I was without it. Don't get me wrong, the whole point of the essay was to point out how the "shameless" sinverguenzas of my family were really acting out to save us all. It is impossible to imagine how radically altered our lives, their lives, my mother's life would have been by not being buried in shame and literally "muriendonos de la verguenza." So imagine my surprise, when Latina/os, in reckless and careless statements and asides recreate that shaming. Someone once asked, "So is that all you know how to write?" A little further along in my maturity I responded, "I promise to stop writing about Puerto Rican drug addicts when there are none left." But the first time I was shamed like that it was a forty-year-old Puerto Rican man and I was twenty-two and we were the only two Puerto Ricans in the room, the only two writers of color for that matter, and I didn't write again for five years. Pero ya tu sabes, shut one faucet in the kitchen, but you can still pull water in the tub.

Of course all of this is happening under a myriad of gazes. The white gaze. The male gaze. The gaze of class and respectability. All of us are operating within a kaleidoscope of intersectional identities that make a phrase like "a people" a very difficult thing to grasp or hold or see clearly. Yet, community, and the communal, is a deep need for survival and safety. For a writer there is also the reality that you can never quite belong to the people you most love and come from, at least not in the same way, once you start writing about them. Perhaps it is because you never quite belonged that you ever write in the first place. The most wounding is when someone, judging me based on the alleged "quality" of my English or my Spanish or my face or I have no idea what, decides that can't possibly be my life experience and accuses me of writing what white people want to read about us. I have entered the phase of life en que "Lo Que Diran la Gente" matters to me almost not at all. Almost. Except for the people who always matter because they are yours. Because they are mine and they will always matter.

Llave #5

Water/truth spilling in and out from several directions is hardly the bull's eye I have in mind when I set out to write an essay, but each condensed distraction is leading faster to unraveling why I have to keep writing around what there is to say. You might coin the term a poetics of obfuscation. Pa' que tanto hablar? Pa' que tanta' palabra'? The very same streets of the Bronx that made me strong, made me who I am, also destroyed my parents. It is the mystery at the core of my life. Why them and not me when I had so many markers in place for that downfall according to all the good studies about what happens to kids who grow up like me. How do some of us become blood price so that others might go free? Why do some of us live in the beast and get fully digested, while others escape through an eye or an ear and live to tell the story? It is a question that plagues me and terrifies me as my sons become men.

Llave #6

You don't want to hear about Puerto Rican drug addicts from the Bronx and neither do I. You can't possibly be more exhausted or frustrated or irritated by this story than I am, than they are. No one has paid more than they have for the sins of our longing to look away and get on with proving how good "we" really are and how bad "they" are. How we are the norm and they are the exceptions. Choices. Personal responsibility. No one to blame but themselves. I've been there and felt it. All of it. All the stages of grieving over and over again for all the near-death experiences of parents living entire lives on the edge. Angry is my favorite one. Denial a close second. I have never been anywhere near acceptance.

I also know it's bullshit. I am not some exceptional exception to the rule of their self-destruction. Un milagrito of good choices and good behavior. People will ask in awe meant to be a compliment, "Wow, but how can you be how you are coming from that?" First, I say "I don't know" and then I say but "I suspect my parents are just like me." They look shocked. Buried beneath those ruins are the seeds of who I am. How can it be otherwise? I look like them, I dance like them, we all three love Orchard Beach and Central Park. What time bomb went off in them that didn't go off in me? I don't know. The new heroin crisis in white communities has everyone, including the NYTs, looking for causes and reasons because "these were good kids." It is a public health crisis. My parents were never given that benefit of the doubt. Then, because I write and because I teach creative writing at Bronx Community College, I have to ask myself the question: How can I both illuminate their fall and their grace? How can I tell the story of us, not the story of me versus them or me surviving them? How do I tell the story of me emerging through them? How can I help my students do this as well? Maybe we could invent a poetics of disruption.

Llave #7

When Audre Lorde writes "Poetry is not a luxury," I hear story is not a luxury and I hear truth is not a luxury, and it all comes clear. I have no interest in telling my story, our story, to perpetuate myths or stereotypes, and I certainly don't need or long for pity, though compassion is always warmly received for we are all the walking wounded with a story that needs to be respected and honored. I need to add our story to the quality of light by which I can scrutinize our lives and give names to the nameless, so it can be thought. I am never writing about Puerto Rican drug addicts or drug dealers or people on welfare. I am always writing about lost sons and daughters and mothers and fathers and brothers and sisters and best friends. I am writing about the people I have most loved and been loved by, however imperfectly, which is I think the only way any of us know how to love. I am writing about myself. I am writing to imagine our triumph, but I cannot do it without first documenting how we were brought to our knees. We could, I think, aim for a poetics of thriving, if we could be less afraid of the way the path there might make us look.

ON READING, AND SHAME

Sasha Pimentel

I've been trying to understand why, as a Filipinx poet, I'd found myself more drawn to Black and Jewish American voices in poetry than Asian and Pacific Islander American voices over my development as a writer. It's been a source of private shame for me as I've stood in the front of classrooms, a professor, extolling to younger writers of color how they *need to know the conversation, what they're writing into*, or in my office as I've pushed books into my students' hands. This late question entangles my present shame into the shame I already know, have always known, the different shames I have learned to live with as if they were my little brothers and sisters. This, in and of itself, is a kind of grappling that is specific to writers of color, how we define who we are to ourselves and to others because those contours aren't taught to us by our white mentors—because, like many writers of color, I've had two forms of education in reading: my public one and my private one.

I'm guessing almost everyone else in this anthology has an intimate relationship with the practice of reading, and I do too: it's my longest safe relationship. Jericho Brown, in his poem "Again," writes:

> *My father loves his wife*
> *and the shape of her body*
> *even if hunched in retreat,*
> *their son keeping up. I'm so sick of it—*
> *another awful father*
> *scarring this page too—*
> *a bruising scratch.*

Like Brown's speaker, I too am so sick of it, my father another awful father scarring even this page in the book you are holding—my father another father slipping up from under your pressed palms where you did not expect to find him, his body growing and bending to the curve of your forefinger as you use it to follow this type. But then Brown says:

> *We walked back*
> *through an open door.*

Because the poem unfolded like this,

> *and again I am bundled*
> *in cousin Kenny's clothes*
> *from last school year*
> *my hand held by my mother's.*
> *We walk as if the house behind us*
> *isn't warm enough*
> *for my feet. In the dark*
> *we make a few blocks*
> *around the one-story neighborhood*
> *that I loved*
> *though nothing I've written*
> *tells you this.*

we know that the open door this child and mother walked back through was the same door through which they had first tried to leave, but just like that, we are pulled back to our homes—even if violent—because they are our homes.

In my own home, my brother and I were allowed one hour of television a day, which my brother as the elder got to choose, which was always *Robotech* or *Teenage Mutant Ninja Turtles*. The periods when my father was absent, my brother and I walked home from school in Connecticut, New Jersey, Georgia—we moved almost every year—in puffed jackets and boots whose tips darkened with snow, to our rented house where my mother was always crying. The adult Sasha considers this woman, my mother, who was loved by her parents, who had a gentle father, whose mother (smelling of imported fish) met my young mother in Sampaloc to press into her hands cash for her tuition, my mother who'd wanted to be an oceanographer but for her family's small business was told to study accounting, my mother who'd met my father on her first accounting job in Makati and had hated him, but then one night he stood between her and the door's exit, the steel lintel framing his darkening curved body, then he swept her into a taxi, the luxury of a taxi in Manila.

And just like that, a goat mewled, his hooves stepping above and into the wet earth of the Ilocos as my father's family fasted him for slaughter. The adult me—the one who knows this because my mother told me, she raised me to these stories before bed as she rubbed the bruises that streamed my body, Vicks VapoRub scenting our air and its quiet brutality, our American air conditioning groaning into the clouds from the humidifier and her voice like rain—the adult me knows that she'd asked my father to feed that goat, to make it stop, his yowls and whines shuddering the night, but my father had said, *let him cry*, then he took her to Saudi Arabia and cloaked her with an abaya.

My father ferried us all to the U.S. after, was more traditional than my mother, so he took away her car even in a new country, where she couldn't legally work anyway. So when my brother and I came home, we only knew my mother's closed bedroom door and the sound of her crying, quotidian as afternoon storms in the tropics, our child bodies wrestling quietly out our own angers, my brother and I encircled on the carpet spitting and punching each other, but silently, so as not to bring out our mother, my brother and I flushed with each other and the rhythm of our hidden moaning mother.

When my father lived at home, we didn't wrestle. We chose separate corners of the house to tuck paper into itself as origami. I dismembered my Barbie dolls, grafittied their flat pelvises and soft faces. Our mother cried openly at the dining table then, told us with her hands flat on the glass how badly she'd wanted to die but we existed, how we stopped her from brooking her freedom by the fact of our sweating bodies. But before my father came home, she wiped her face, pinched her cheeks back. We all scurried to pick up the remnants of our play and our living. Then, my brother and I laid ourselves face down, hinged our bodies onto the edge of our parents' marital bed for our daily whipping.

In the United States, my father confused words like *bitch* and *beach* with his accent, his children sometimes said *mm-mnh* or *uh-huh* instead of *no, Papa* or *yes...*, so his belt uncoiled; some nights it kept unrolling beyond the 6 o'clock hour. I'd say something too pointed, or not know what it is I said or didn't say, so my father punched my head into the embroidered sofa as I fainted in and out of his blows. The more my body grew, my crevices sweltering, the more Dan Rather's voice became a beat I heard on the den's television, the nation's news like distant waves, my mother becomes a blurred figure at the edge of the carpet, her hands fumbling one over another as she stood at the end of the room: my mother having forgotten how to plead as my father's body wound a semi-circle over mine, my father telling my mother with his words said quietly to my body, *whore, slut, bitch* finally with the unstressed vowel, that he chose me over her to touch this way, so *let her cry*.

But what we were allowed, generously, were books. Once a week, my father in his own kindness took us to the library, told us we could check out up to 12 books a trip. Jericho Brown says: "And why don't I mention / he kissed my forehead / before covering me / on the couch that was my bed?" and too: "I should have told you this / lines ago." Yusef Komunyakaa in "My Father's Love Letters," writes:

> *On Fridays he'd open a can of Jax*
> *After coming home from the mill,*
> *& ask me to write a letter to my mother*
> *Who sent postcards of desert flowers*
> *Taller than men. He would beg,*
> *Promising to never beat her*
> *Again. . . .*
> *Words rolled from under the pressure*
> *Of my ballpoint: Love,*
> *Baby, Honey, Please.*
> *. . . .*
> *My father could only sign*
> *His name, but he'd look at blueprints*
> *& say how many bricks*
> *Formed each wall. This man,*
> *who stole roses & hyacinth*
> *For his yard, would stand there*
> *With eyes closed & fists balled,*
> *Laboring over a simple word, almost*
> *Redeemed by what he tried to say.*

And Robert Hayden, with all his wisdom in "The Whipping" of how whippers must purge what they have had to bear, how the whipper too must lean, "muttering against / a tree, exhausted" could also summon, in "Those Winter Sundays," this kind of father:

> *When the rooms were warm, he'd call,*
> *and slowly I would rise and dress,*
> *fearing the chronic angers of that house,*
>
> *Speaking indifferently to him,*
> *who had driven out the cold*
> *and polished my good shoes as well.*
> *What did I know, what did I know*
> *of love's austere and lonely offices?*

It was my father, who played chess with me and sang opera while he cooked, who gave me reading. So I read Shakespeare, all of the plays, *Les Misérables*, *Lord of the Flies*, *Great Expectations*, *The Iliad* and *The Odyssey* by the time I finished fourth grade. These were the dead, white writers my white teachers, who, titillated to have in me the model immigrant minority, folded into my palms as they clasped their hands over mine, before they asked me from my wrists and forearms unburied from my cuffs why I seemed so "accident-prone." I can tell you, though if you're reading this you already know it yourself, the secret shuttered life of reading, how badly we seek refuge in it, other walls, other places, find in those stories for ourselves other bodies. But I can tell you too that when I discovered Alice Walker's *The Color Purple* in the public library, I fell down in the stacks to the industrial blue carpet because I recognized something in Pa, and confused myself in Celie. Celie wrote in her diary: "Dear God, I am fourteen years old. ~~I am~~ I have always been a good girl."

I suppose I have constructed in you too a sort of reader I'm writing an imaginary letter for now, as if on the onion skin of air mail paper, like I were still writing to the Philippines, to my sweet aunts and grandparents. You are not the formal Dickensian *Dear reader! It rests with you and me, whether in our two fields of action, similar things shall be or not*, us colluding which characters we can leave on the hearth and in a scene, as if we were powerful, could just "Let them be!" You are the grandparents and aunts who raised me in our iron-gated house in Las Piñas before my visa was finally approved, my mother and father with brother sweeping back to the Philippines where they'd left me from ages one to seventeen months. According to my mother, we emigrated for Saudi as a family the day before Manila International Airport shut down because Ninoy Aquino Jr. was murdered.

You are the delicate voices of my distant family, rising and falling in the rain while we unearth the ginger. You are who, I realize now, I've spent—getting to you only through flights, blue-and-red-dashed mail and the ripple of the telephone's long-distance—less than five years of my life with, physically, and the other thirty in adopted countries dreaming. You are who I really loved, am imagining still alive.

You see, it was in the words that Black male poets wrote, not white ones, where I found the kinds of fathers I recognized. But it was in the stories of Black women writers where I found women, and daughters—women I could make into my own. Alice Walker, Maya Angelou, Nella Larsen, Jamaica Kincaid, Zora Neale Hurston, they were who I found furtively in those sticky public libraries, whose books I hid under titles like *The Hobbit* and *Ender's Game* so my father wouldn't sight them. I hid their paperbacks on my tented legs behind my algebra textbook, so when my parents looked through the required open door into my bedroom, it would look like I was studying. It was my own form of study, beyond parents and teachers. I hid them because I knew these books were changing me into someone in that house I wasn't allowed to be—and as Janie drew the horizon in around herself, her cloak a crescent around her body, these characters and authors became aunts who through books I could touch with my very hands.

But I was ashamed then to feel what stirred in my body. Ashamed to love the dark body.

If I accidentally tanned too much, my mother whopped me with her tsinela before she washed me with rubbing alcohol or bleaching soap. And my father, when he was home, asked me at night before I had to kiss him if I'd pinched my nose up 100 times to try to draw out from my Pinay face a Roman architecture. (I'd forgotten this, or had normalized the experience, until I was talking to the poet Patrick Rosal at a conference the other week, and learned not every Filipinx family had asked such things from their children).

I may have been a child when I immigrated *here*, but I aged with the sharp consciousness that we did not belong. That our bodies were allowed in the United States only by virtue of my father's H-1B Visa, and after, our pink "Green Cards" stamped with the words "Resident Alien." I knew I had to shut myself into the polyethylene chairs and laminate boards of school desks, to contract quietly there, because at any time I could be caught being "un-American," I could be deported. We were conscious we were foreign, of the anomaly of our shortened brown limbs and our kinked black hair. With the shame of our private trespasses, my parents gifted me the shame of assimilation in the great hope of the shame of citizenship.

We have a concept that is often said with a hand over the mouth and a wag of the finger: "ang kapal ng mukha." It means how dare someone, the gall, how thick her face must be to bare herself without her community's honor, as if to "lose face" is to lose it by submerging it under too thick a skin, or masks. It is a concept meant to shame an individual's audacity—or her lack—to norm her into her community's values.

It's taken me years, and I suspect decades more, of pulling in writers of color *who dare speak* as my horizon, as my own close constellation enough to slough off such a face. To create my own new community where speaking, against curses or silence, is valued. It's taken the belief of giants like Philip Levine and Gregory Pardlo advocating my work before I could see how in APIA writers' faces I sighted too quickly my own vague face, so wanted to reject them because I'd confused their art with my own shuddering, my family. I think it is taking me this essay now, talking to you because of Luisa Igloria, to see, specifically in Filipinx faces, features that don't make me wince in learned response, don't lasso me right back into my father's chest and his warm breath, his hand heavy and small on my college-aged breasts in Manila. It has taken me much too long to unlearn how to untangle from other APIA writers' stories, a face and a body which, if it looked too much like mine, I'd wanted to sit in a bathroom with, holding a bottle of rubbing alcohol to scour it clean.

I wish I had that kind of tender, coadunate immigrant's story.

The kind Ocean Vuong had in the essay "The Weight of Living: On Hope, Fire Escapes and Visible Desperation"—before his uncle's suicide, before the shape of emptiness made itself so visible, it became inescapable. The kind where we could gather over oiled noodles and a pig's slack mouth on the table, and as we flaked the meat from above his rigid hip say to each other, *this, yes,* this *was what all that loneliness was for.* That we waited for hours after holiday dinners each taking turns holding the phone until we could connect across the Pacific, for *this.* That our chests hitched when those calls came from the other side, when we heard our people's voices, gauzy, trembling, wobbly, how they hesitated after the lady said, "Will you accept this collect?" and we knew one more of us was sick or dead. For *this.* That my father found himself in a country where both women and men were taller than him, white men in their perceived friendship leaning their forearms onto his head or shoulder the way one might rest upon a tall counter, for this. My mother hidden into the house for decades for this. My brother's body in the shadows, and my body twisting, for this. We would eat the animals we'd roasted, suck the noodles for prosperity and long life, behold the bounty, then put down our Corelle plates and our single beers for our patriarch to offer the sum, and his accounting, of our unit's immigration.

In this dream, my father's hands blow open to say, *I have given you everything. My father, my mother, my little brother Dante I held my own body over to protect him from my father—all gone, just like that—*(in a wink, a snap, my mother's voice on the phone to me now, stinging, "you didn't know your Tito Dante was dead? Heart attack. It's because you don't call, 'Sha") *while I worked here to raise you. I have given you this life soft with paper towels, food and air conditioning. So I gave you too the part of myself which hurt.*

But to have that kind of thanksgiving, I would have to go home, to walk back through that open door through which I've already left. I would need to ignore how our gatherings are made over slaughter. My family's lies so private, they never even needed to say them. My father's tongue, darting in and out of a circle of bone marrow. And his words that took me until adulthood and my own parenting to learn he must have spoken as a kind of Morse code, hoarse signal of his own anguish. The nights I know sensations from memories so incomplete, my own story can only be the minority story.

When I lived in my parents' houses, I'd misplaced the feeling that something was wrong in my home with that soaking feeling of "alienness" that comes with being an immigrant. I confused what was local to my family to something larger in my culture because it's what I knew, was told by the present agents of authority was "Filipino"; I didn't know that not all mothers teach their daughters my mother's stories. What to say when they ask you about the bruises. What to do when they find you after you'd run away from a report card with less than A pluses (you were so scared of the coming beating), and how your neighbor, Fatima, had held you, pulled you from your mother in front of the sirens to comb your tangled hair with her fingers, to ask you as she held your cheek if there was something wrong, anything you'd wanted to tell her, before you'd looked at her face creased into an origami of asking, Fatima who needed you to say it out loud, before you remembered your mother's words.

I think maybe I've been drawn to Black and Jewish American poets, particularly narrative poets, because of how plainly they are able to tell difficult stories. The unspeakable breaches of body, pain, somehow compassion, all of it together: words and paper bobbing just above grief. And how such grief is so large, ensnared in a human shame more incomprehensible than just a girl's and her family's, you cannot look away. Though I value the undertaking of language poets (I believe such writers are pulled to those forms so they might decolonize the languages of their own colonization), I think as a writer I still need new stories, or new ways to tell the same story. I need the scene, the narrative. Perhaps I still need to change the shapes of the words which were formed for the hollow of my mouth to find words which feel more true. Philip Levine advises: "to me, mythologizing is really a subtle way of saying you're lying. But you're only being dishonest to yourself. You construct a kind of history, a fabric, that in a way protects you from the past and its harsher, more difficult moments. A lot of this technique has to do with constructing one truth and then wiping it away with a second one. It's the process of writing: you start with a truth, and you break through to a deeper one."

I wonder if I've become some sort of sad curator of my experiences to you now, if as words I am blurring in your hands into the thin skin of this paper, just another crouching daughter, another lousy father. My private stories no longer so private are "preserved for time without end. . . . on view / in a glass room," my inner life an artifact you might cradle like a mosquito trapped in amber as in Dorianne Laux's poem "The Last Days of Pompeii."

I never made it back to my grandparents' house. Cancers, bankruptcies, martial laws have shuttered their windows into a place I can only re-enter through imagination. But I have two more poems to write you from, Tita, aking Lolo, Lola, miss na miss kita, the first Paisley Rekdal's "Happiness," which begins:

> *I have been taught never to brag but now*
> *I cannot help it: I keep*
> *a beautiful garden, all abundance,*
> *indiscriminate, pulling itself*
> *from the stubborn earth: does it offend you*
> *to watch me working in it,*
> *touching my hands to the greening tips or*
> *tearing the yellow stalks back, so wild*
> *the living and the dead both*
> *snap off in my hands?*

When my childhood dimmed and clicked shut too, in my early twenties I moved to Fresno to study poetry. Franny and Phil Levine let me go to their house to help in their garden on the weekends one season. I cut thorned branches down with Franny, who taught me to shear back the bodies of dewed bushes so they would bloom. At the end of each of those Sundays, Franny pressed into my damp hands a white envelope with two crisp twenty-dollar bills, as if she were my grandmother. I still plant tomatoes each year, even in desert El Paso, for what Franny has taught me.

Rekdal continues:

> *I can wait longer than sadness. I can wait longer*
> *than your grief. It is such a small thing*
> *to be proud of, a garden. . . .*

That first year in graduate school, I walked the Levines' garden in circles with Franny, watched her pluck from the boughs the ripened fruits each tree could bear. Phil came outdoors too once, watched us cage in the tomatoes. Talking a little of poetry before he went back inside to work, he told me, "you don't need to be depressed to be a poet, Sasha, just observant." Kwame Dawes said, in a question-and-answer forum I attended recently in Miami, "I'm not faithful to what I know as a poet—I'm faithful to what I know as a human being. What do I dare? . . . . giving dignity to the everyday individual, looking for the elegance in the people around me, looking for the beauty—and beauty is not always pretty—beauty can be brutal, but it's that looking, looking for the language to give to what moves me."

Levine, who was an extraordinary and exquisitely direct man, the poet I most admire, writes a poem with a language that truly moves me in "The Mercy." About a grandmother and her immigration, the poem's voice courses holy as flood:

> The ship that took my mother to Ellis Island
> eighty-three years ago was named "The Mercy."
> She remembers trying to eat a banana
> without first peeling it and seeing her first orange
> in the hands of a young Scot, a seaman
> who gave her a bite and wiped her mouth for her
> with a red bandana and taught her the word,
> "orange," saying it patiently over and over.
> . . . .
> "The Mercy," I read on the yellowing pages of a book
> I located in a windowless room of the library
> on 42nd Street, sat thirty-one days
> offshore in quarantine before the passengers
> disembarked. There a story ends. Other ships
> arrived, "Tancred" out of Glasgow, "The Neptune"
> registered as Danish, "Umberto IV,"
> the list goes on for pages, November gives
> way to winter, the sea pounds this alien shore.
> Italian miners from Piemonte dig
> under towns in western Pennsylvania
> only to rediscover the same nightmare
> they left at home. A nine-year-old girl travels
> all night by train with one suitcase and an orange.
> She learns that mercy is something you can eat
> again and again while the juice spills over
> your chin, you can wipe it away with the back
> of your hands and you can never get enough.

A poem too, or a story, can be, for a girl in shame, a mercy. She can read it again and again. Can never get enough.

Sasha's Incomplete List of Writers to Turn to, For Other Lonely Children

Albert Abonado
Chinua Achebe
Ai
Neil Aitken
Rosa Alcalá
Elizabeth Alexander
Sherman Alexie
Kazim Ali
Maram al-Masri
Ivy Alvarez
Maya Angelou
James Baldwin
Rick Barot
Tara Betts
Arlene Biala
Elizabeth Bishop
Sherwin Bitsui
Merlinda Bobis
Jorge Luis Borges
Carlos Bulosan
Gwendolyn Brooks
Jericho Brown
Dino Buzzati
Toni Cade Bambara
Italo Calvino
Truman Capote
Nick Carbó
Cyrus Cassells
Paul Celan
Cathy Linh Che
Chen Chen
Frank Chin
Marilyn Chin
Steven Church
Kate Chopin
Billy Collins
Eduardo Corral

Edwidge Danticat
Kwame Dawes
Toi Derricotte
Emily Dickinson
Rita Dove
Mark Doty
Oliver de la Paz
Junot Diaz
Natalie Diaz
Camille Dungy
Nathan Englander
Martín Espada
Jeffrey Eugenides
Peter Everwine
Tarfia Faizullah
Lawson Fusao Inada
Sesshu Foster
Evelina Galang
Sarah Gambito
Roxane Gay
Shirley Geok-lin Lim
Amitav Ghosh
Allen Ginsberg
Eugene Gloria
Louise Glück
Jorie Graham
Jessica Hagedorn
Kimiko Hahn
Corrinne Clegg Hales
John Hales
Lorraine Hansberry
C.G. Hanzlicek
Joy Harjo
Robert Hayden
Terrance Hayes
Seamus Heaney
Juan Felipe Herrera

Lee Herrick
Edward Hirsch
Maxine Hong Kingston
Garrett Hongo
Marie Howe
bell hooks
Langston Hughes
Zora Neale Hurston
Amanda Huynh
David Henry Hwang
Luisa A. Igloria
Kazuo Ishiguro
Randa Jarrar
Major Jackson
Honorée Fanonne Jeffers
June Jordan
Allison Joseph
Janine Joseph
Franz Kafka
Jamaica Kincaid
Milan Kundera
Stanley Kunitz
Yusef Komunyakaa
Jerzy Kosiński
Nella Larsen
Dorianne Laux
Li-Young Lee
Joseph O. Legaspi
Primo Levi
Philip Levine
Federico García Lorca
Audre Lorde
Ada Limón
Anne Marie Macari
Adnan Mahmutović
Mike Maniquiz
David Mas Masumoto
Dunya Mikhail
Brenda Miller

Janice Mirikitani
Toni Morrison
Dipika Mukherjee
Alice Munro
Haruki Murakami
Marilyn Nelson
Aimee Nezhukumatahil
Bich Minh Nguyen
Achy Obejas
Sharon Olds
Cathy Park Hong
Gregory Pardlo
Octavio Paz
Carl Philips
Claudia Rankine
Bino Realuyo
Paisley Rekdal
Barbara Jane Reyes
Adrienne Rich
Alberto Ríos
Tony Robles
Lee Ann Roripaugh
Patrick Rosal
Arundhati Roy
Benjamin Alire Sáenz
Nicky Sa-eun Schildkraut
Sonia Sanchez
Bienvenido Santos
sam sax
Natalie Scenters-Zapico
Liz Scheid
Gary Shteyngart
Delmore Schwartz
Tim Seibles
Ravi Shankar
Brenda Shaughnessy
Naomi Shihab Nye
Patricia Smith

Zadie Smith
Art Spiegelman
Gerald Stern
David St. John
Ira Sukrungruang
Arthur Sze
Wislawa Szymborska
Eileen Tabios
Bryan Thao Worra
Natasha Tretheway
Jon Tribble
Brian Turner
Luís Alberto Urrea
Mai Der Vang
Ocean Vuong
David Foster Wallace
Alice Walker
Cornel West
Colson Whitehead
Elie Wiesel
Richard Wilbur
Lex Williford
Susan Wood
C.D. Wright
Richard Wright
Ishle Yi Park
Karen Tei Yamashita
Monica Youn
C. Dale Young
Kevin Young
R. Zamora Linmark

BECOMING THE WEATHER: REFLECTIONS ON POETRY AS CULTURAL, POLITICAL, AND SPIRITUAL ACT

José Angel Araguz

My initial reading of Sandra Cisneros almost did not happen.

In high school, I read T. S. Eliot, Yeats, and e. e. cummings as part of the official curriculum. The only writers of color encountered were in the form of novels and non-fiction essays. One in particular, Rudolfo Anaya's *Bless Me Ultima*, was read with extreme mixed feelings on my part. His story of a young boy's coming of age and to terms with his cultural background in New Mexico is, in hindsight, a powerful and necessary story. What I responded to then, however, were the things I recognized: the italicized Spanish words; the poverty; the presence of violence as part of the landscape inside and outside the home; the faith in folklore, mythology, and religion. Despite this recognition – or perhaps *because* of it – I read Anaya's novel with what I can only term as a mix of embarrassment and resentment.

Looking back at this moment, I see that the main issue is that no one had prepared me for the sociologically well-intentioned yet uncomfortable experience of "diversity." Looking back, I did not know about diversity as an addendum to curriculum, did not know that an effort was being made on my behalf to include me. After so many years of not being included in the literature read in classes, suddenly there were faces I knew. And it terrified me. It, ironically, *alienated* me. Not only because of the recognition, but because Anaya's story was not my own.

I grew up in a household where, yes, I spoke Spanish, but anything like cultural pride ended there. Anaya's characters went back and forth between languages fluently, and lived in small, close-knit communities in New Mexico. I grew up in a city of strangers, called in by the hushed tones of my mother and aunt who had me translate bills for them in South Texas, parents who asked me not to share stories about the rest of the family who lived in ranches and makeshift shacks in Mexico. So, in many ways, rather than feel included, I felt exposed, singled out, while at the same time doubly excluded. Some part of me then had an inkling of the decisions made for me, of the weather set in motion, and rejected it. While I cannot say when I decided to be a writer (I could point to several acts of faith and omens early on, but no outright moment of *click*), I remember that part of my reaction to reading Anaya was: *If that's how I will be expected to write, then I'll have none of it.*

All this changed, or, rather, I was forced into an uncomfortable reconsideration when I was introduced to the poetry of Sandra Cisneros. I knew her then as being famous for *The House on Mango Street* (which I pointedly did not read until grad school because of the aforementioned experience with Anaya), and so was surprised when my high school Spanish teacher introduced me to the book of poems *Loose Woman* for outside reading. With their mix of Spanish and English, passion and bitterness, these poems moved me to fall further in love with language as well as challenged me to try to match their ambition and intensity in my own poems. Before I could put up any defenses about discomfort, I was swept up. Whatever made these poems work, I wanted in. I wanted to wield the two languages given me like the speaker of "Dulzura," who spoke in riddles and demands:

> *Make love to me in Spanish.*
> *Not with that other tongue.*
> *I want you* juntito a mi,
> *tender like the language*
> *crooned to babies.*
> *I want to be that*
> *lullabied,* mi bien
> querido, *that loved.*
>
> *I want you inside*
> *the mouth of my heart,*
> *inside the harp of my wrists,*
> *the sweet meat of the mango,*
> *in the gold that dangles*
> *from my ears and neck.*
>
> *Say my name. Say it.*
> *The way it's supposed to be said.*
> *I want to know that I knew you*
> *even before I knew you*
>
> (Loose Woman 27).

Cisneros's poems were unabashedly emotional and direct, the exact opposite of the poems I had been exposed to up until then. Here, the italicized Spanish is charged with meaning, each phrase of affection another piece of evidence as the speaker makes her case. But I did not understand it that way then. What kept me reading beyond the charge of cultural and emotional recognition was how much the writing showed how the writer herself loved language.

Seeing as the lesson for me of the *Loose Woman* poems was one of voice and of owning my sense of self, culture, and literary heritage, I was surprised to find, years later, that Cisneros had to overcome similar issues as I had in order to write them. In regards to the Chicano/a writers of "El Movimiento," the politically-motivated artists and community activists of the 60's and 70's, Cisneros states in an interview:

> ...[early] in my life, Chicano writers didn't appeal to me. I have to admit now as an older poet, an older writer looking at these early Chicano writings, they still don't appeal to me very much. I can acknowledge them and their importance historically and socially and see where they were coming from, but I don't think that the best Chicano writing came out of that period. I think a very emotional voice and social voice came out of that time with a real need to create Chicano identity and so they're important to me in a historical sense, not in a literary sense... [Latinx] writing has shifted so that it's meant to reach an audience via books as opposed to simply via public rallies... Technically the work is tighter and stronger now. Also, it's much more exciting to me as a woman because the subjects and voices that we're hearing are voices that we never heard before. I didn't feel any sense of identity and I did not feel emotionally moved when I read those early Chicano writers. They didn't have anything to say of my urban experience or my experience as a woman and I could read them and just throw them away (Torres 213-214).

Coming across this statement nearly twenty years after my experience with Anaya and *Loose Woman* was instructive for me; not only did it let me off the hook for my discomfort with Anaya's book, but it also showed me how to reconcile those earlier feelings with a humbler and more generous sense of consideration. When Cisneros talks of reading early Chicano/a writers and then being able to "just throw them away," she is talking about a practice that every writer regardless of cultural background has to go through. One must read through their predecessors and the weather their efforts have established, then go against that weather in order to add to it.

In keeping with my early, bristling self, in college I refused to read only Latinx writers; I kept my Yeats, and added to him Pablo Neruda, Federico Garcia Lorca, and

Alejandra Pizarnik, balanced with Charles Simic, Sharon Olds, W. H. Auden, and Naomi Shihab Nye. As much as my reading widened, however, I could not ignore the difference felt in reading someone like Auden, who I love for his breadth of prosodic invention, versus someone like Neruda, whose poems often faced up at me in both Spanish and English, on opposing pages. Studying Auden was counting syllables and identifying meter; with Neruda, I had to choose to either trust a translation (which, despite the respective merits of Merwin and Bly, I could never fully embrace), or I could muscle out the words for myself, which was its own unnerving task. Unnerving, because reading Neruda and other Spanish language poets meant having to face the fact that I grew up *speaking* and not *writing* or *reading* in Spanish. What was on the page was far from the intimacy and recognition of my conversations back home (and even those are still mocho, choppy). What was on the page was literary, and, like a college degree and Auden's metrical wit and stoicism, was yet another thing to be earned and challenged by.

I recognized the distinction of this reading "stand-off" of sorts in a comment made by Demetria Martinez regarding her feelings on writing primarily in English:

> *It was only later in life that I had a chance to learn Spanish. I can hold my own in conversational Spanish, but I'm not totally fluent. I read a lot in Spanish. To do so is a cultural, political, spiritual act. I want to be able to influence my nieces and nephews, to encourage them to love languages (Torres 88).*

Note what comes up for Martinez in discussing Spanish: the "cultural, political, spiritual"; "nieces and nephews"; a "love" of languages. Reading a Latinx writer, whether it be a Barnes & Noble-canonized great like Neruda or a contemporary poetic bilingual wizard like Urayoán Noel, has never been a light matter for me. Whole worlds come up with these texts.

For the longest time, I could not read another Latinx writer without some sort of mixed reaction. When I came across a writer I felt was not genuine, using Spanish words as ornamentation or bringing in cultural markers to exoticize themselves, I would bristle; yet, I also found myself reading some of the same writers with an awe tempered by envy. What had they figured out to reach success, both in publication but also, and more importantly, in aesthetic expression? How had they gained access to a sense of self that spoke with conviction of the whole person? What exactly went into that? What about my schooling – from high school to a PhD in creative writing – kept this side of my writing at bay, kept me mistrustful? What was I lacking? What am I made of?

In my near twenty years of a writing life, it is this questioning energy that remains a constant. Whether bristling against something new or being swept away by it, the weather of being a poet raised in the United States informed by literary traditions in both English and Spanish has been one filled with movement. Over time, I have learned to accept this state of being unsettled, to read the weather project by project. I offer no apologies for the confused, truculent high school kid I was, but rather point to the shift in perspective. My story is not one of denying culture, only to return to it later; rather, it is a story of being another thorny manifestation of it.

Much of the work of accepting the particular bilingual stew my writing exists in had to be done outside of the creative writing *work*shop. In workshop, I got direct feedback on my overuse of prepositions, but sometimes rolled eyes, sometimes questions in response to the use of Spanish phrases. Again, it was shaped by the notion of weather, of feeling compelled to either bristle or respond with the wind of my voice. For this reason, these brief reflections occur in the worlds outside of workshop as well: my reading, my writing, my explorations of self. I find myself echoing Martinez in finding myself engaged in "cultural, political, spiritual" acts that no classroom can prepare one for.

Notes

Cisneros, Sandra. *Loose Woman*. New York: Alfred A. Knopf, 1994. Print.
Torres, Hector A. *Conversations with Contemporary Chicana and Chicano Writers*.
    Albuquerque: University of New Mexico Press, 2007. Print.

A RADICAL POETICS OF LOVE
(A BENJAMINIAN ESSAY ON *INVISIBLE MAN*)

Khadijah Queen

When writers work toward the opposite of detachment, toward an encompassing of unruly feelings through a process of definition and inclusion that allows us to create abundantly and invent freely, a kind of solidarity with language occurs. That solidarity fosters an acceptance of emotional articulation via an imaginative process of examination, which allows us to question what we think we know via how it feels to know it. To feel is not weakness, but strength. This empirical and theoretical poetics essay advocates for critical engagement based on radical love, rooted in womanist thought. If any worthwhile exercise has at its root a desire for deeper understanding and connection, and if criticism's main motive is inquiry, the radical part comes in the form of a wider questioning than intellectual, to include the physical and the emotional within the intellectual as an attempt at completeness. It may ultimately fall short of such completeness, but it may also move further than lines of inquiry which aim to exclude; a poetics of love that works as the opposite of narrowing—rather, as an encompassing that centers on the capacious notion of love: that "we are each other's / business" in the Brooksian communal sense; that "we are each other's / harvest."[1]

If one aspires toward the collective good in a humanist rather than a Marxist way, then where does the ego move or quiet or activate in a reader when triggered by a text to investigate once-fixed ideas? Can we make an equation of time, experience, prior reading and the unquantifiable element that is awareness/consciousness? When it comes to that ego movement, where does the ego set itself aside in the body? How does awareness of that movement function as a feeling alongside thinking, and alongside the act of making? What does love have to do with that, with writing, with poetics, and what does it mean?

A radical poetics of love defines love as a self-love, both the specific and broadly applicable self to be sure, but also a love of future-making, of possibility, even if or because it is or seems futile. Far from a fetish for the foolish, it rejects the recklessness of cynicism in favor of a future that, if we can imagine, we can ultimately create as a new reality if we pay attention to how we feel when we read and write, radically and rigorously. Rigor, in the context of a poetics of love, means inquiry—thorough, diligent, exhaustive—avoiding the negative connotations (i.e. rigidity, severity or discomfort) of the word in favor of a relentless investigative questioning. Rigor mortis, for example, describes the stiffness of a dead body—but a poetics of love assumes and operates from life, and aims to function as part of a whole self.

Indeed, it must be said that just as the mind is a powerfully creative living instrument, so is the body. To ignore that, even in literature, is to ignore humanity—and thus to be at cross-purposes to that literature. As demonstrated in Ralph Ellison's *Invisible Man*, in which the narrator's body is turned into metaphorical negative space, the body's absence results in a grotesque existence built of unmediated observation, a terrorism of consciousness, a hyperlucidity sans outlet. The energy must have somewhere to go. It might even expand outside of body, mind, place, all the way out to the larger universe, a way of connecting that has everything to do with the intersection of time, how it repeats itself in us, linking the past and present and future in an endless loop.

In his essay "On the Mimetic Faculty," Walter Benjamin points out that "in the remote past the processes considered imitable included those in the sky [...] Allusion to the astrological sphere may supply a first reference point for an understanding of the concept of nonsensuous similarity."[2] If we look at *Invisible Man*'s astrological chart[3], we see eerie parallels to what we already know, emphasizing an extant wholeness alongside the artificiality of separation. Besides having several planets in bombastic fire signs like Aries and Sagittarius, the ascendant is in Gemini, and the ascendant in astrology dictates how the individual appears to the world. For *Invisible Man*, that means interest in "intellectual activities, humanism, and abhorrence of violence, constant doubt of all mental concepts, hesitancy and academic interest."[4] The resemblance of the chart to the novel is uncanny. But, what does such apparently esoteric knowledge have to do with a radical poetics of love? You can't love yourself if you don't know who you are, and astrology is a connective insight into the self alongside one's possible place(s) in the universe.

What does that have to do with literature? Maybe nothing; maybe everything. Ellison, in a 2014 audio interview aired on NPR, recalls his thoughts on reading: "When I was a kid, I read English novels, I read Russian translations and so on, and always I was the hero. I identified with the hero. Literature is integrated, and I'm not just talking about color or race. I am talking about the power of literature to make us recognize, and again and again, the wholeness of the human experience."[5]

Our aims as writers, then, are not separate from our aims as humans: connection, understanding, knowledge, and, yes, love—of self, of others, of the world—and the body is a key. Importantly, the novel begins with a material recounting of the physical elements of the narrator's makeup: "I am a man of substance, of flesh and bone, fiber and liquids—and I might even be said to possess a mind. I am invisible, understand, simply because people refuse to see me."[6] Ellison's novel asks: How do we reconcile a material self with the material world's negation of that self? What do we lose when we lose a self? What do we gain when we lose an externally imposed self? What does the truth cost us to know? Must it be our very existence? The nihilism at the heart of the novel at first appeared to have no love in it. In considering a radical poetics of love, reading for that love is part of reading generously: what do the characters love? Does that love have substance, or is it a regurgitation of what they're told to love, a surface type of repetition, a mechanical habit born of cultural or family programming? Does the author show love for the story, language, or individual elements of the piece in how it's constructed? Those questions assume that love is not a frivolous concern, but that it lies at the heart of the discourse on text construction, on literariness, on beauty, and on the relevance of a work to the larger human story within the field of literature.

If a radical poetics of love exists or can exist in that field, how does beauty function at the intersection of love and poetics? In terms of *Invisible Man*, beauty is not only in the story but in the language of the text, how it is formed or crafted by the author. Even when the content consists of harrowing and horrible scenes arguing the opposite of beauty, the language demonstrates arresting qualities and conjures images that resonate far beyond the tumultuous era in which Ellison wrote it. Passages like one early in the book describing the "hole" where he lives lets the reader ruminate on appearances both visual and cultural, although beauty functions most often as an illusion and a danger throughout the novel itself:

> *My hole is warm and full of light. Yes, full of light. I doubt if there is a brighter spot in all New York than this hole of mine, and I do not exclude Broadway. [...] Those two spots are among the darkest of our whole civilization—pardon me, our whole culture (an important distinction, I've heard)—which might sound like a hoax, or a contradiction, but that (by that contradiction I mean) is how the world moves: Not like an arrow, but a boomerang. [...] I have been boomeranged across my head so much that I now can see the darkness of lightness. And I love light. Perhaps you'll think it strange that an invisible man should need light, desire light, love light. But maybe it is exactly because I am invisible. Light confirms my reality, gives birth to my form.*[7]

Thus, at the intersection of the love the narrator expresses, the beauty with which it is expressed, and the difficulty of the content is a literariness that has retained its compelling quality over many decades, partly because it connects seemingly disparate ideas and makes room for the simultaneity of contradictions—a wholeness, which Benjamin Harshav also makes room for: "The trouble with many definitions of literariness or aesthetic definitions of art was that they wanted to subsume it all under one principle or in one linear model […] while we are dealing with *multidimensional objects with changing and optional forms on all levels and in all aspects.*"[8]

What does contradictory-or multidimensional-content-as-wholeness have to do with a radical poetics of love, though? Just as it looks for the presence of love, it looks as well where love is absent. In *Invisible Man*, notably, there is no love for women. There's lust, there's fear, there's a mild and somewhat fond appreciation, but no love. The dancing white woman at the beginning is sinister and seductive, representing an oft-repeated ideal that is a bit heavy-handed, but perhaps necessarily so for the sake of the time period. A womanist reading of the text, however, demands attention to the male narrator's conflicted feelings toward and rather simplistic depictions of the female characters.

The women in the novel are not referred to or discussed in true human terms, and thus become thin archetypes. We have the nurturing mother figure in Harlem, Mary (again, a little heavy-handed with the symbolism); we have the stripper/whore at the battle royal on page 19, dehumanized and caricatured ("The hair was yellow like that of a kewpie doll, the face heavily powdered and rouged, as though to form an abstract mask, the eyes hollow and smeared a cool blue, the color of a baboon's butt"); and later, the wealthy (and married) seductress, who calls emotion "primitive."[9] One could argue that the novel isn't "about" the women, but the narrator's interaction with them (and/or lack thereof) is central to the revelation of his situation, his character. The women function as tools used to show the narrator's state of mind, to move the story forward, to symbolize the dichotomy of desire and repulsion, of possibility and impossibility. While the narrator's fear of his desires takes center stage, the women's desires appear nonexistent, incidental or speculated upon, often ungenerously. Particularly glaring at the beginning of the novel is the reverently and exotically described blonde dancer, with the narrator beset by contradictory feelings at the sight of her naked form: "I wanted at one and the same time to run from the room, sink through the floor, or go to her and cover her from my eyes and the eyes of others with my body; to feel the soft thighs, to caress her and destroy her, to love her and murder her."[10] One cannot, then, use a poetics of love fully without talking about the counterpoint of fear, and its fraternal twin, violence.

How do fear and violence operate in a novel, outside of authorial intent but within the text itself as part of a modernist zeitgeist, subconscious or otherwise? A poetics of love might argue that one way it manifests is as fear of love or attachment (the spiritual implications of which this paper will avoid for the sake of brevity). Thus the common American trope of the alienated man, for example, for whom women serve as symbols of the American Dream (or nightmare) and function as props to plot rather than as complex individuals with their own identity crises to attend to, arises from a fear of love as much as it does a struggle against a rigged system. It means, often, that more than half of the population continues to be silenced or suppressed in literature because of their portrayal as complicit, accessories in a system that men, in fact, created—making a destructive loop. It also means we don't know the whole story, or what the postmodern might be like if we did know these women characters in singular novelistic ways on a larger scale. In a futuristic American (or indeed human) narrative, women must exist as more than markers of occasions or sidebar plot devices. We can be critical of the American imagination, with love; we don't have to accept it the way it is. Inclusion is simply another word for accuracy, and another positive aspect of rigor.

Speaking of inclusion, or the lack thereof, the extended detour at the Trueblood property again highlights the absence of love, especially for women, and exposes just how deeply destructive that absence is. Trueblood's daughter Matty Lou's silence and unintelligibility, along with his inscription of dream and memory onto his act of sexual violence toward her, exemplify the justifications for the ancient and still rampant abuse of women. Further, Trueblood embodies Mr. Norton's insinuated fantasy of raping his own daughter, which, structurally, it is the point of the side trip to illustrate.

And speaking of detours, here it's important to digress into a brief discussion of narcissism. The narrator's self-interest and self-obsession is staggering, and could be considered his fatal flaw. He cannot crawl out from the depth of his self-concern, his obsession with what he believes to be a chance to elevate his station in life: "I identified myself with the rich man (Mr. Norton) reminiscing on the rear seat."[11] The narrator is desperate for the wrong things, albeit with a desperation born of the basic need for survival: acceptance by white benefactors and the precarious privileges that entails. And more than that, he also wants respect. He wants validation as an orator, a scholar, and at the most elemental level, as a man and a human being: an ontological state he cannot arrive at in a society that functions completely counter to that desire. Indeed, without the inner knowledge and conviction of his own humanity as manifest by the mere fact of his existence, as opposed to outside recognition, he enacts an erasure of himself that mirrors his invisibility to the white benefactors he so ardently and repeatedly tries to impress in the novel. His pursuit, however, though he cannot see or articulate it, is also a pursuit of love; he wants to be loved and accepted.

Invisible Man tells us that the absence of that love perverts humanity and that the damage of such an absence is total and inescapable for all parties involved. In the

Trueblood section, Mr. Norton's sober insistence that his fate is tied to the Black students of the college, and the narrator in particular, isn't an exaggeration. The young narrator's misunderstanding or slow understanding of that concept speaks to his youth, but also his misguided identification with Mr. Norton. Not only does the encounter with Trueblood upend such identification, but it uncovers deep fears, insecurities, and further exposes his precarious position as a Black student vulnerable to the whims of white benefactors. The pretending or masking he endures during the violent battle royal would be for naught if one misstep could ruin his future.

What, then, is the purpose of enduring brutality and suffering under such absurd and persistent conditions? And even more, can a person be visible if they are not truly seen? One answer: not if they are invisible to their own selves. Mr. Norton's hilarious interchangeability among the veterans at the Golden Day shows that, he, too, carries a certain invisibility. He represents more than himself: he represents the oppressor, the absurdity of racism, the pain it inflicts, the traumas it engenders, the chaos it creates. As Edna, one of the Golden Day prostitutes, points out: "These old bastards don't never git enough. They want to have the whole world."[12] In his incapacitated state, Mr. Norton becomes vulnerable to the Golden Day's inhabitants' scrutiny and commentary in a way he wouldn't normally be if at the height of his faculties, although his whiteness still protects him from any real life-threatening consequences.

The narrator, on the other hand, tries to intellectualize his feelings and disembodies the Self in order to integrate his traumatic experiences into memory, in order to function and continue to strive. While it's unclear how much Ellison knew about trauma victims, the elaborate scene at the Golden Day with the veterans strongly suggests that he knew something about Black existence as shell shock[13], as a kind of grief for enduring violence you cannot escape, of figuring out the world *is* actually so absurdly brutal that you decide to give up, or redirect the world from your sight. But instead of doing what the veterans do, drinking themselves into oblivion, the narrator ultimately redirects *himself* from sight in the name of trying to exist in some resigned measure of peace and safety, even from his own rage: "What else could I have done? Once you get used to it, reality is as irresistible as a club, and I was clubbed into the cellar before I caught the hint. Perhaps that's the way it had to be; I don't know."[14]

In a radical poetics of love, one might revise the erased figure in future explorations of Blackness and being toward a sense of self derived inwardly from self-knowing, rather than the narrator's almost pathological examination of the self alongside monolithic whiteness presented in *Invisible Man* and what it thinks, wants, feels, and does. Instead, a self-love based on its existence outside of an institutionalized system of destruction of the individual for the sake of that system's preservation; a self-actualization made possible by a focus on the here-ness of that self as itself, forming under pressure, made powerful by its attention to that ontological formation. If, rather than being lured by the Communist group's flattery, the narrator had instead remained with the Blacks in Harlem, in Mary's welcoming boardinghouse, he may have been able to visualize and actualize himself as a man and as a vital part of a community. As Audre Lorde writes in *Sister Outsider*, "It is not the destiny of Black america to repeat white america's mistakes. But we will, if we mistake the trappings of success in a sick society for the signs of a meaningful life."[15]

But, *Invisible Man* also asks, is it the lot of the African American character to avoid erasure only by existing outside of white-dominated spaces? Is that the only place true visibility is possible? We see the ideological pollution born of segregation in the college's culture, with Dr. Bledsoe fiercely guarding the carefully built and delicately positioned world of the university he runs, made to appear acceptable to the surrounding monolith of whiteness. *Invisible Man* presents the problem of integration as both individual and collective, bringing to how difference confronts the nature of existence. If we assume so-called nonwhite people are, indeed, people in the exact same way so-called white people are, then why don't the cultural and social institutions and environments truly behave in a way that operates on that assumption? In mathematics, we have agreed-upon givens in an equation. If the givens don't sync up between different systems of equations, the problem cannot be solved. Until an ontological agreement occurs, that Black people do exist and are human beings, then it seems the problem of integration cannot be solved, either.

Worth noting further is Ellison's frequent use of symbols that make the case for Blackness as local and global, national and international, personal and political. During the eviction scene, the narrator describes the belongings of newly displaced elderly inhabitants, and being overcome by "a warm, dark, rising whirlpool of emotion which I feared":

> *Pots and pots of green plants were lined in the dirty snow, certain to die of the cold: ivy, canna, a tomato plant. And [...] I watched the white men put down a basket in which I saw a whiskey bottle filled with rock candy and camphor, a small Ethiopian flag, a faded tintype of Abraham Lincoln, and the smiling image of a Hollywood star torn from a magazine. And on a pillow several badly cracked pieces of delicate china, a commemorative plate celebrating the St. Louis World's Fair...I stood in kind of a daze, looking at an old folded lace fan studded with jet and mother of pearl.*[16]

Such internationality is important, since it constitutes a seeing and appreciation of, and participation in, a world that largely seems incapable of doing any better by Black people than to forcibly remove them from their homes in the name of profit, mirroring the reasoning behind the abductions and violent displacement of Africans during the slave trade. But the eviction scene also visually demonstrates that love is Black, and both love and Blackness tend to be met with state regulation and violence—and the fear the narrator speaks of comes from his knowledge of that fact. *Invisible Man* thus maintains that the repudiation, ill treatment, dismissal and persecution of Black people, their bodies and belongings, means that the broader world will remain crueler and lesser for its ferocious incompleteness.

A radical poetics of love acknowledges that radical love cannot exist without consummately human readers, even as both beauty and horror exist, just as both the created thing and the world in which it is created exist. Separating the two might seem a clinical approach, as a surgeon operating on one part of the body in order to assess its function and correct any malfunction, but the surgeon must also account for the rest of the body, how it reacts to a part of it being violated, for surgery is a violation, a cutting into a whole body, despite its reasoning that the excision and/or invasion is for healing purposes. The body bears scars, it changes, it remembers the trauma, it heals but that healing takes time and, as Benjamin writes in *Illuminations*, "a remembered event is infinite."[17]

A radical poetics of love does not shy away from difficult truths. Rather, it pushes difficult and problematic thoughts out into the open, where they can be honestly examined, and hopefully, an evolution toward loving and true solutions can occur. A love-based poetics has no shame, does not worry about whether or not it appears foolish, and lays itself bare in the name of transparency and progression. It is thus fierce, because it naturally opposes views that lean toward separation, which favor using apparent or supposed weaknesses against another party in an attempt to win arguments or to dominate. A radical poetics of love insists there be no domination. In its insistence, it yet worries about its own tendencies toward domination, and questions the need for only one kind of poetics even while it rejects those it finds harmful in favor of its own inclinations. A radical poetics of love acknowledges the simultaneity, and in fact insists upon the wholeness such simultaneity manifests.

Notes

1   Brooks, Gwendolyn. "Paul Robeson." *Family Pictures*, Broadside Press, 1971, p. 19.
2   Benjamin, Walter. "On Mimetic Faculty." Translated by Edmund Jephcott, edited by Hannah Arendt. *Reflections*. Schocken Books, 1978, p. 333-336.
3   https://www.instagram.com/p/BRwjZZuARF8/?taken-by=radicalpoetics Astro.com. Personal Portrait. Inputs: 14 April 1952, 8:00am, New York City.

4   Gemini Ascendant, via Astro.com. https://www.instagram.com/p/BRwkGTFgQxb/?taken-by=radicalpoetics
5   Vitale, Tom. "Ralph Ellison: No Longer The 'Invisible Man' 100 Years After His Birth." *All Things Considered*. May 30, 2014. http://www.npr.org/sections/codeswitch/2014/05/30/317056807/ralph-ellison-no-longer-the-invisible-man-100-years-after-his-birth#http://www.npr.org/sections/codeswitch/2
6   Ellison, Ralph. *Invisible Man*. Random House, 1952, p.3.
7   Ellison, p. 6.
8   Harshav, Benjamin. *Poetics of Exploration*. Stanford University Press, 2007, p.166, emphasis Harshav's.
9   Ellison, p.413.
10 Ellison, p. 19.
11 Ellison, p. 39.
12 Ellison, p. 88.
13 Carten, Alma. "How Slavery's Legacy Affects the Mental Health of Black Americans." July 27, 2015. https://newrepublic.com/article/122378/how-slaverys-legacy-affects-mental-health-black-americans#https://newrepublic.com/article/122378/h
14 Ellison, p.572.
15 Lorde, Audre. *Sister Outsider*. The Crossing Press, 1984, p.63.
16 Ellison, p.270-271.
17 Benjamin, Walter. Translated by Harry Zohn, edited by Peter Demetz. *Illuminations*. Schocken Books, 1968. p.202.

STANDING IN THE SHADOWS OF LOVE: DESIRE AS OBSESSION

Remica L. Bingham-Risher

Desire is obsession, the things we keep going back to, that dig in us, that we dig into. Poetry is about mining—extracting things that come back to us—re-examining love and shadows. When I was married in 2010, I inherited children and extended families and became obsessed with re-examining my upbringing. I started interrogating what I'd learned about love throughout my childhood and how I'd let those lessons move through me. The book that eventually came from all this, *Starlight & Error*, grapples with how all of us collide and come to be and how the mass of what we are—the stars, songs, and voices that guide us—lead to our own reckoning. As desires/obsessions always will, several began to rise to the surface of this work: music, domesticity, God, cosmos, progeny. All the things that seem to converge the night Rumain is killed.

When I am revising, wrestling with the overt sweetness of *Starlight & Error* (one-sided nostalgia, too much romance, mothered and mothering, all stacked chronologically), I am knocked back into reality when one of my oldest and dearest friends is shot by police. On Dec. 2, 2014, on his doorstep with a pill bottle in his pocket and Happy Meal in hand for his daughter beyond the door, Rumain is next in a long line of the taken. One headline reads, "Eric Garner, Mike Brown and now, Rumain Brisbon: White Officer In Arizona Shoots And Kills Unarmed Black Man."[1] That day in December, Rumain became one more on the growing list of black men gunned down (mostly by police) that led to the Black Lives Matter movement: July—Eric Garner, August—Mike Brown, October—Laquan McDonald, November—Tamir Rice, December—Rumain Brisbon. Boy who journeyed with me from middle school, through three states, past college, his phone calls and thick letters filled with photographs, Chicago love and wild chuckling; boy close as a kin, now gone.

In the chaos of the next few weeks, there are many sleepless nights and so I won't wake my husband lying closer than usual (as he is worried for me, I am frightened for him and we both fear for our son sleeping in the next room) I wear headphones lying awake in bed, letting music spin and spin, voices moving in and out of focus.

As soul music is an obsession that resides deep in me, I am often writing in the voices of those who skipped over vinyl each Saturday morning in my parents' home. In Patricia Smith's introduction to my second book, she calls colored girls a definitive, lost tribe, then names me among those who honor black nostalgia, saying: "She gravitates toward the addictive sugar of soul music, follows the gospel of Smokey and the Temps until she realizes how gorgeous their lies were"[2] and this is maybe the greatest compliment I have been given in all my natural life. Assonance, sparse enjambment, repetition and end rhyme make their way into much of *Starlight & Error* because, in subtle ways, I am trying to emulate popular song. Here's an early poem in the book where I'm really just trying to channel one of the greatests, Stevie Wonder:

If It's Magic

When I find the Songs in the Key of Life *45s*
I marvel at the messages my parents inscribed:

Sweet Dee and Junior Bee—In Love '79
their marks on the sheath's concentric circles,

inside, on the lyrics booklet, worn smooth
their scratches on the grooves.

I spend a year playing the set
enthralled every few days by some new epithet—

a background voice trailing,
a tone's shift or timbre—

my mother counts the years since their beginning,
how I interrupt their ending,

heartache and revelry,
what each of us remembers.

Such strange obsessions I inherit:
their soulful cinders, indecipherable

refrains, this awful insistence
on fraught and ordinary pain.[3]

As music informs much of this work, I turn to other poets—like Patricia Smith, Honorée Fanonne Jeffers, A. Van Jordan, and Mitchell Douglas—as models for how to embody the electric energy of soul and, of course, I go back to song because it usually soothes me. But when Rumain dies, no matter what book I carry to bed or which tracks blare through my headphones, I am restless and afraid. I am so new at being a mother, at living with the double-fear that black men carry as a weight balanced atop my own young black woman's already triple fear, not to mention having to balance this with hope and a brave face, for my small son's sake who is still, as Smith puts it "sweet in that space between knowing and not knowing."[4] One poem in Starlight & Error, "Our child is not yet ten and we are clearing his closet", is about me literally throwing away the hoodies from my son's wardrobe in desperation, as if that will solve anything at all.

How strange it is to realize in the days after Rumain's death that, once and for always, we are no longer children. Sometimes I forget how much time has passed between experience and memory. Amidst my grief, I write about losing time. In the poem "Solstice", I am a still-point and my children—like me—have lost their trust in time, in anyone:

> *When you discover you are old enough*
> *that nothing has novelty*
>
> *you live with teenagers*
> *who've learned*
>
> *little more than to abhor everything*—I hate Daylight Savings Time.
> I hate Virginia. I hate being here.
>
> …
>
> *If we can steal their light and time*
> *without warning*
>
> *what joy is there to be had,*
> *what can they love without fear?*[5]

I met Rumain when I was around 13. That year, I kept a journal, every day for 365 days. Since then, I'd rarely looked at the massive blue binder kept on the lowest shelf of one of my bookcases. When Rumain is killed, I crack the binder open looking for remnants of who we were, who he was, as opposed to what people begin imagining. Rumain, the closest friend I had from seventh grade until college, who moved from

Chicago to Phoenix and landed at Challenger Middle School when he arrived. A year older and infinitely wiser, he always laughed when I'd strut over (was my fearlessness then boldness or naiveté, even now I can't be sure) to make an inquiry no one else would. The girls sent me to find out who the cute boy was in the Bulls jacket the first day he arrived.

Reading my journal, I find so much happened that year: my uncle died, I prepared for high school, I loved a boy and lied to him about it (the man I would later marry), Rumain and I became best friends. He watched over me like a brother, asked about my chorus recitals, gave me teasing nicknames, rapped Tupac's "Dear Mama" to his mother on Mother's Day. Our marathon phone calls got me grounded more than once—our inside jokes and late night meandering, equally boy and girl crazy both of us, trying to figure out who we'd like to become. We whispered in the dark, behind the backs of our mothers for countless hours that year and many years thereafter; we grew up together and in spite of ourselves.

Tucked into the pages of that old journal are letters and photographs we sent back and forth for at least a decade. I lay them on my living room floor and cry most of the night after he is killed. In the morning, when I am brave enough to read them, I find Rumain was all the light I remembered—silly and solemn, funny and cocky as any teenage boy with all his natural insecurities can be—very little of the myth people quickly begin to craft.

When your friend becomes a flashpoint, with everyone clamoring for one side of the story or the other, what's strangest is most everything people say about them is myth. Back in Phoenix, my husband's cousin calls to tell us, "They're making your boy out to be Scarface or somebody," which is to say, we are in the 21st century but it is still better to eviscerate some men than for anyone to admit *we've made a mistake* or say *we're sorry for what we imagined*. One letter he's written to me is from 1997, a few months after we've both left Phoenix for a time. In it, I find what's left of Rumain's voice when he writes:

> *Are you missing me yet? Cause I'm missing you like crazy. It's like ever since I left Phx I haven't had any one to talk to, and knowing that when I do go back you won't be there just hurts my feelings. But you know what, I ain't gon' trip cause I know at least one day before this life ends we will see each other again. I really don't have much to say besides I miss you and I can't wait 'til I see you again, and that I love you with all my heart. Shorty, I hope you like the picture. P.S. Don't get too close to your new homies cause can't nobody replace me. Do you want to know why? Well I'll tell you why cause you ain't never had a friend like me.*[6]

The world is mourning a man and I am mourning a little boy, an almost man, a man becoming. I search for pieces of him everywhere. What I find is never enough.

*

A few days later, I am back on the living room floor, re-reading letters. Laying against a shelf, mouthing the words I'm reading, my son finds me, puts his hand on my shoulder and asks, "Mom, are you alright?" I must look something like Hannah to Eli, drunk with grief. He is so perplexed, so earnest and confused. I do this so infrequently—wallow in sadness out in the open—that it must seem to him like something has gone very wrong. I feel terrible putting on a smile and saying I'm alright, but what else can you tell a nine-year-old who is in between video games and has found you here so unlike yourself?

Like most parents, I worry that I might be ruining him and write the lines "no child has ever learned / by anything other than mimicry"[7] in a poem that will eventually become "Skipping Stones" in *Starlight & Error*. I can count on one hand the times my son has had to be grown up, and I am weary the world will make him one sooner than I want it to. Once when I was a few years older than him, my parents were screaming in the living room, something they rarely did. When I couldn't stand it anymore, I rushed in with my fists clenched and yelled, "Stop it! You're killing me!" and it startled them so completely they began apologizing, first to me, then to each other, but the damage was done: I'd already seen them for part of who they were—flawed and helpless—and they'd already recognized who I might become: growing mirror, unsteady and gazing, like my son.

So when the Four Tops' rendering of "Standing in the Shadows of Love" spins from the shuffling on my playlist in those weeks of mourning, it is no wonder I hear their rough pleading and get stuck. Amidst the police brutality and rioting, the odd disturbance looming over my own house, I suddenly hear this familiar not as a man longing for his woman but as a mother supplicating her fallen son:

> *Didn't I treat you right, now baby, didn't I?*
> *Didn't I do the best I could now, didn't I?*
>
> *So don't you leave me*
> *Standing in the shadows of love*
> *I'm getting ready for the heartaches to come*[8]

I let the song repeat for hours then *days*; I am obsessed with the ugliness of desire to the point of suffering. When writing, I've found it best to fight obsession by trying to climb into it at its core. Hence, while my boys are sleeping, Rumain's family is making plans to lay him to rest, and the Four Tops missive is still spinning, I scour the Oxford English Dictionary for the etymology of the word "shadow" and, among other things, I find:

- *Comparative darkness*
- *A phantom; a faintly surviving renown*
- *What is fleeting or ephemeral*
- *Image cast by a body intercepting light*[9]

I write inside and around these ideas throughout *Starlight & Error*. In the poem "*Regents Prompt: What are the best ways for step-parents to deal with the special problems they face?*", children are a haint and harboring, mothers are "bound by the weight [they]'ll cradle."[10] In the poem "Noble & Webster, Shadow Sculptures", "Our house is a mess of musk and sawdust--/...keels and scrim and kin/ caught in the net of our limbs", "illusions stacked into a kind of mortality."[11] I am stuck on the difficult thing: how do we keep living beyond our fear? How do we save what's coming? In the difficult landscape of the present, is black love revolutionary? Are faith and forgiveness? How do we transcend the mistakes of those who made us? Can music save us? Can the stars?

I write a poem in hopes of getting inside this obsession—this helplessness that accompanies mothering and aging, that is always the underlying foundation of grief, what we didn't say to and for the missing. Poems are also the place I can continue to question God, in my faith and the persistent difficulty of maintaining it in such a violent world. In the poem, and in the book as a whole, I try to do many things: enact the horror that accompanies death, the oft unmentioned ugliness and ruining of a perfectly good body; I move from metaphor to literal to lyric trying to encapsulate the many pathways to death or roadblocks to keeping the living; and finally, I address how death transforms the mothers too—how they are often blamed for what happens to their children by our judgment and questioning. This is truer in the case of these 'martyr children' like Trayvon or Mike Brown or Rumain, created by the social upheaval surrounding their deaths, then suddenly demanding activist mothers, women who must rearrange their whole lives to keep 'doing' for children they no longer get to keep. And what of the generations who carry the weight of all this? Here's the poem:

Getting Ready for the Heartache to Come
or A Body Intercepting Light

Ps. 39:6 – Surely every man walks about like a shadow.

Grief is a half-sung ballad
  the mothers I've known are bellowing
into stilled ears or stitches
  in the sewn up backs of blue-black boys.
There are various sites of trauma:
  wombs, needles, pipes, badges,
ropes unraveling, all wavelengths of visible light,
  prison fights, the Devil's busy hands.
Bodies aimed when they leave
  like bullets or planes, rarely become letters,
tulips, fireworks, any welcome opening,
  rarely live as good, as free, as long
as we hope. The women enduring this
  must become: saints or blameworthy,
miracles or memories. The Bible says men
  are gods or gleaning but mothers shelter
the in-between: ghost-children wandering the streets
  of every generation—father-god, son-god, holy-
spirit—flexing in photo albums, toys in the curio,
  lighters, guns and flasks carved
with initials, all the left-behind things
  gathered around a table, mothers
singing, Didn't I do the best I could, didn't I?[12]

Once it is written, I am at least freed from the Four Tops and move on to other fixations. My overarching hope for *Starlight & Error* becomes a desire—an obsession—with proving, in our work and life, LOVE (layered and crafted memory) CONQUERS FEAR. And, truth be told, you are reading this now because, after being married, being a mom, losing a best friend, and trying to be ready to guide others through losses that will come, I've realized how important it is to be free to say what I'm afraid of out loud, to dispel it; to show my children, that even in unimaginable times, we can create our own way out of fear. In living, in writing, there is, ultimately, nowhere else to turn but my deep abiding faith in things bigger than all of us and our desires. Smith closed her introduction to my second book by saying: "Colored girls know one thing more than they know anything else, and that is that a God is real and present, hurtling through our blood, blessing us every dawn with a blank canvas upon which to sing."[13] I sing in this shadow, in every desire, I hope to be: a body intercepting light.

Notes

1. (Dec 4, 2014). Eric Garner, Mike Brown and now, Rumain Brisbon: White Officer In Arizona Shoots And Kills Unarmed Black Man. Headlines and Global News (HNGN). Retrieved from http://www.hngn.com/articles/51824/20141204/eric-garner-mike-brown-now-rumain-brisbon-white-office-arizona.htm
2. Bingham-Risher, Remica L., *What We Ask of Flesh*, (Wilkes-Barre, PA: Etruscan Press, 2013), xv.
3. Bingham-Risher, Remica L., *Starlight & Error*, (Doha, Qatar: Diode Editions, 2017), 12.
4. Smith, Patricia. (2011). Pearl, "Upward." In E. Danticat & R. Atwan (Eds.), *The Best American Essays 2011* (pg. 180 – 184). New York, New York: Mariner Books.
5. Bingham-Risher, Remica L., *Starlight & Error*, (Doha, Qatar: Diode Editions, 2017), 55.
6. Brisbon, Rumain. Personal Letter. Received by Remica L. Bingham-Risher, 10 October 1997.
7. Bingham-Risher, Remica L., *Starlight & Error*, (Doha, Qatar: Diode Editions, 2017), 56.
8. Holland, B., Dozier, H. and Holland E. (1966). "Standing in the Shadows of Love" [Recorded by The Four Tops]. On *Reach Out*. [Album]. Detroit, Michigan, Motown. (1967)
9. Shadow. (2017). In *Oxford English Dictionary Online*. Retrieved from http://www.oed.com
10. Bingham-Risher, Remica L., *Starlight & Error*, (Doha, Qatar: Diode Editions, 2017), 37.
11. Ibid., p. 54.
12. Ibid., p. 34.
13. Bingham-Risher, Remica L., *What We Ask of Flesh*, (Wilkes-Barre, PA: Etruscan Press, 2013), xv.

NIGHT WALKS:
ON ADDICTION, ADOLESCENCE AND ART MAKING

Ocean Vuong

Dear Ma,

I am writing you because it's late.

Because it's 10:52 pm on a Tuesday and you must be walking home after the closing shift.

I'm not with you 'cause I'm at war. 'Cause it's already March and the president wants to erase my friends. It's hard to explain.

No, it's like this, for the first time in a long time, I'm trying to believe in heaven, in a place we can be together after this blows ~~over~~ up.

They say every snowflake is different. But the blizzard covers us all the same. A friend in Norway told me a story about a painter who went out during a storm, searching for the right shade of green, and never returned.

I'm writing you because I'm not the one leaving, but the one coming back, empty-handed.

//

You asked me once what it means to be a writer. So here goes.

Seven of my friends are dead. Four from overdoses. I am twenty-five years old, an age none of my dead friends have reached.

Take the long way home with me, Ma.

Take the left on Walnut, where you'll see the Boston Market where I worked for a year when I was 17. Where the Evangelical Christian boss fresh from Pakistan never gave me any breaks. Where, hungry on a 7-hour shift, I would lock myself in the broom closet, stuffing my mouth with cornbread I had snuck in my black, standard-issue apron.

I am 5 ft 4 in. tall, 112 lbs. I am handsome at exactly 3 angles and deadly at at least 17. I don't celebrate my birthday anymore.

Trevor was put on OxyContin after breaking his ankle doing dirt bike jumps in the woods a year before I met him. He was 15.

OxyContin, produced by Purdue Pharma in 1992, is an opioid, making it heroin in pill form.

I never wanted to build a "body of work," but to preserve these, our bodies, breathing and unaccounted for, inside the work.

Take a left on Emmets Rd., where all that's left of the house that burned that summer during a thunderstorm is a chain-linked dirt lot.

The truest ruins are not written down. The girl grandma knew back in Go Cong, the one whose sandals were cut from the tires of a burned-out Army jeep, who was then erased by an air-strike three weeks before the war ended—she is a ruin no one points to.

After a month on the Oxy, Trevor's ankle healed, but he was a full-blown addict.

//

In a world myriad as ours, the gaze is a singular act: to look at something is to fill your whole life with it, if only briefly. Once, at 14, crouched between the seats of an abandoned school bus in the woods, I filled my life with a line of cocaine. A white letter "I" glowed on the seat's peeling leather. Inside me, the "I" became a switchblade—and something tore. In minutes, I became more of myself, which is to say the monstrous part of me got so large, so familiar, I could want it. I could love it.

The truth is none of us are enough enough. But you know this already.

In that gutted bus I laughed among the skater kids laying on the paint-chipped metal floor. The drugs had blurred their bodies so that, for a moment, I didn't feel Asian and alone, but like a person beside other people. And the night equalized us further by obscuring our faces. Like black gauze around a cut.

It took me seven years to get clean. Sorry.

The sentence is a linear object—but thoughts are not lines. Memory returns, and to recall is to fill the present with the past. The cost of remembering, then, is life itself.

I murdered myself, for I have remembered.

//

It's been six years twenty-three days since I used but I made that number up.

The truth is the last time I relapsed, back in 2010, I said fuck it. Said I'm not gonna count the days anymore, but simply be *inside* them—yes—like words in a book.

The truth is I only came here looking for a reason to stay.

Sometimes those reasons are small: the way, sitting on the roof of a doorless shed, the 7 pm sun in late August turns the fine hair on a boy's cheek the color of low flames. The smallest brushfire in the world, you think, on the left side of his face. How you couldn't look away, aching to be the brief god of that country—so that it burns for you and no one else.

Or the way you pronounce spaghetti as "bahgeddy."

The truth is we enter language the way we entered ourselves, alone.

The truth is I'm scared the need to use hasn't left me.

It's late in the season—which means the winter roses, in full bloom along the national bank, are suicide notes.

Write that down.

//

I'm writing you at the speed of light and blood. That is, I am writing in the voice of an endangered species.

You once said, "The human face is language-less—but tells you the truth." You read faces closely because you can't read.

"I feel bad for Trump," you went on, watching the President on TV, "even when he's smiling he looks constipated."

The one thing I've been my entire life is a son. That can't be nothing.

I wanted to tell you that—but instead I texted you a smiley face.

You responded, hours later, with a photo of a bowl of squash soup you had just made.

They say nothing lasts forever but they're just scared it will last longer than they can love it.

Are you there? Are you still walking?

The truth is I'm scared they will get us before they *get us*.

Tell me where it hurts. You have my word.

If you're reading this in your next life, know that I'm writing you in a time without safe spaces. A time where, to live, we had to learn to charge the finite surface of a body with the capacity for safety, which, it turns out, is to be perpetually in motion. The sooner you learn to sing while dodging, the longer you will stay here. It shouldn't be this way. But you should stay here. You should sing.

My words, they're so still on the page, but on good days, they outpace the bullets.

That's a lie. Writing didn't save me, it just kept me busy enough for the years to hold me in place, breathing.

Cocaine, laced with oxycodone, makes everything fast and still at once, like when you're on the train looking across the fogged New England fields, toward and beyond the brick Colt factory where my stepdad works, you see the rusted dome of a silo—parallel to the train, like it's following you, like where you're from won't let you off the hook.

Our bodies are the unlegislated archives of ghosts. To be alive is to be an unpillaged library.

You taught me that. You taught me by breathing.

//

Back in Hartford, I used to wander the streets at night by myself. If I couldn't sleep, I'd get dressed, climb through the window—and just walk. At night, my body could exist in a public space on its own terms, without judgment, without otherness. Out there, in the endless oily concrete, I was beyond anonymous; I was no one.

Some nights all I would hear was an animal shuffling, unseen, behind garbage bags, or the wind suddenly strong overhead, a rush of leaves clicking down, the scrape of branches from an oak out of sight. But mostly, there was only my footsteps on the pavement, or the dirt on a baseball field under a few stars, or the gentle brush of grass on a highway median.

Until one night I heard someone praying.

Through the lightless window of a street-level apartment, a man's voice in Arabic. I recognized the word Allah. I knew it was a prayer by the tone he used to lift it, as if the tongue was the smallest arm from which a word like that could be offered. I imagined it floating above his head as I sat there on the curb, waiting for the soft clink I knew was coming. I wanted the word to fall, like a screw in a guillotine, but it didn't. His voice, it went higher and higher, and my hands, they grew pinker with each inflection. I watched my skin intensify until, finally, I looked up—and it was dawn. It was over.

Salat al-fajr: a prayer before sunrise. "Whoever prays the dawn prayer in congregation," said the prophet Muhammad, "it is as if he had prayed the whole night long."

I want to believe, walking those aimless nights, that I was praying. For what I'm still not sure. But I always felt what I wanted was ahead of me. That if I walked far enough, long enough, I would find it—perhaps even hold it up, like a tongue at the end of its word.

//

First developed as a painkiller for cancer patients undergoing chemotherapy, OxyContin, along with its generic forms, was soon prescribed for all bodily pain, even ones as mild as muscle spasms and arthritis.

This mass prescription of the pill was no accident. There are only so many cancer patients, which means there is only so much profit the drug producer can make off that demographic.

Using a multi-million dollar ad campaign, Purdue sold OxyContin to doctors as a safe, "abuse-resistant" means of managing pain. The company went on to claim that less than 1 percent of users became addicted. This was a lie. By 2002, prescriptions of OxyContin for non-cancer pain increased nearly10 times, with total sales reaching over $3 billion.

Trevor was into *The Shawshank Redemption* and Jolly Ranchers, Call of Duty and his rescue Border Collie, Mandy. Trevor who, after an asthma attack, said, hunched over and regaining his breath, "I think I just deep-throated an invisible cock." Trevor was a boy who had a name, who wanted to go to community college to study Physical Therapy. Trevor was alone in his room when he died, surrounded by posters of Led Zeppelin. Trevor was 22. Trevor was.

//

Once, at a writing conference, a white man asked me if destruction was a necessary prerequisite to art making. His question was genuine. He leaned forward, his blue gaze deep and wrought under his black cap stitched with '*Nam Vet 4 Life*, the oxygen tank connected to his nose hissing beside him. I looked at him the way I do every white veteran from that war, thinking he could be my grandfather, and I said no. *No, sir, destruction is not necessary for art.* I said that, not because I was certain, but because I thought my saying it would help me believe it.

But why *can't* we fathom creation without annihilation, without going to war with ourselves? Why can't the language for creativity also be the language of regeneration?

You killed that poem, we say. You're killing it, man. You're a killer. You came in to that novel guns blazing. I am hammering these words, I am banging them out, we say. I owned that workshop. I shut it down. I crushed them. We smashed the competition. I'm hunting for the right phrase. I'm wrestling with the muse. Can you crank up the volume on the beheading scene, please? The violence was a bit melodramatic—was it really that bad? The state, where people live, is a battleground state. The audience is a target audience. *Good for you, man*, a man once said to me at a party, *you're making a killing with poetry. You're knockin 'em dead.*

The question, then, is how do we speak of life, celebrate it, without using the language of death? If we cut ourselves off from our bellicose roots, can we still be replanted; can we thrive without forgetting that the edge of the wound is also a hem?

//

The truth is we don't have to die if we don't feel like it.

Sorry, just felt like saying that.

One afternoon, while watching TV with Lan, we saw a herd of buffalo run, single file, off a cliff, a whole steaming row of them thundering in technicolor off the mountain. "Why do die themselves like that?" she asked, her mouth open. Like usual, I made something up on the spot, "They don't mean to, Grandma. They're just following their family. That's all. They don't know it's a cliff."

Staring into the screen, she said, "Well maybe they should have a stop sign, then."

We had many stop signs on our block. They weren't always there. There was this white woman named Marsha down the block. She was overweight and had hair like a lesbian rancher, a kind of mullet cut with thick bangs. She would go door to door, hobbling on her diabetic leg, gathering signatures for a petition to put in stop signs in the neighborhood. She has two boys herself, she told Ma at the door, and she wants all the kids to be safe when they play.

Her sons were Kevin and Kyle. Kevin, two years older than me, overdosed on heroin. Five years later, Kyle, the younger one, also overdosed. After that Marsha moved to a mobile park in Coventry with her sister. The stop signs remain.

That was then. This is now. And you and I, we are the last part of now—which means there's no stopping.

//

My doctor, rubbing his five o'clock shadow, suggested that addiction, in many cases, could be linked to bipolar disorder. It's the chemicals in my brain, he went on. I got the wrong chemicals, Ma, or rather, I don't get enough of one or the other. They have a pill for it. They have an industry. They make millions. Did you know people get rich off of sadness? I want to meet the millionaire of American sadness. I want to look him in the eye, shake his hand, and say, "It's been an honor to serve my country."

I don't want my sadness to be othered from me just as I don't want my happiness to be othered. They are both mine. I made them. And what if—what if the joy we feel is not another "bipolar episode" but something we fought goddamned hard for? Maybe I jump up and down and kiss you too hard on the neck when I learn, upon coming home, that it's pizza night because sometimes pizza night is more than enough, is my most faithful and feeble beacon? What if I'm running outside because the moon tonight is children's book huge and *ridiculous* over the maple line, the sight of it a cool sphere of medicine?

What if, when all you have been seeing before you is a cliff, and then this bright bridge appears out of nowhere, and you find yourself running even faster across, knowing that, sooner or later, there will be yet another cliff on the other side? What if my sadness is actually my most brutal teacher? And the lesson is always this: You don't have to be like the buffaloes. You can stop. You can wait until there's more land. Because as long as you're on earth, there's always more land.

There was a war, the TV man says, but it's "lowered now."

Yay, I say, swallowing my pills.

//

At my worst I was down to ninety-two pounds, a Black and Mild hanging from my lips and my head empty all night under the Route 2 overpass. It was 2007. You driving through the dark streets looking for me, Lan in the passenger, his pinched pale face peering through the window, a bag of Burger King with a veggie burger and small fries for me, cold in his lap.

The truth is my recklessness is body-width. Always has been.

Once, the anklebone of a blond boy underwater.

There was a greenish light in that line and you saw it.

The truth is, if the inside of my mouth tasted like Jolly Ranchers, I wouldn't kiss nobody ever again.

There was a lie in that line and you saw it. Keep walking.

The truth is we can survive our lives, but not our skin. But you know this already.

Get at me.

//

I woke one night to the sound of wings in the room. It sounded like a pigeon had flown through the opened window, its body thrashing against the ceiling. I switched on the lamp. As my eyes adjusted, I saw Trevor sprawled on the floor, his sneaker kicking against the wall as he rippled under the seizure. We were in his basement. We were in a war. I held his head, foam from his mouth spreading down my arm, and screamed for his Daddy. That night, in the hospital, he lived. It was already the second time.

I never did heroin because I'm scared of needles. When I declined his offer to shoot it, Trevor, tightening the phone charger around his arm with his teeth, pointed between my feet with his chin, "Looks like you dropped your tampon, little one." Then he winked, smiled.

What if art was not measured by quantity but ricochets?

What if art was not measured?

If they come for me, ~~take me home~~ take me out.

The one good thing about national anthems is that we're already on our feet, and therefore ready to run.

The truth is one nation, under drugs, under drones. Get at me.

The first time I saw a man naked he seemed forever.

He was my father, undressing after work. I am trying to end the memory. But the thing about forever is you can't take it back.

Let me stay here until the end, I said to the lord, and we'll call it even.

Let me tie my shadow to your feet and call it friendship, I said to myself.

//

In 2005, Johnson & Johnson began the distribution of a synthetic version of heroin called Fentanyl (the drug attributed to the death of Prince). Fentanyl is 10 times more potent than street heroin and can kill the first time it's used. Because of this potency, more and more heroin is being laced with Fentanyl.

Horror story: "Johnson & Johnson: A family company."

Horror story: hearing Kevin's voice when I close my eyes at night four years after he died.

He's singing Nina Simone, whose music I introduced him to, the way he used to sing it—suddenly, between lulls in our conversations, his arm hanging out the window of the Chevy, tapping the beat on the red exterior. *Humankind is overflowing / And I think it's gonna rain today.* I lay there in the dark, mouthing the words until his face appears, young and warm and enough.

I wake up, lunge for the phone.

The black sparrow this morning on my windowsill: a charred pear.

That meant nothing, but you have it now.

//

Take a right, Ma. There's the overgrown field where one summer I watched Trevor skin a raccoon he had shot with his granddad's Smith & Wesson, his teeth by then the green of glow-in-the-dark stars in daylight. On his truck bed the animal's pelt rippled in the August breeze. A few feet away, grained with dirt, a pair of eyes, stunned by the sight of us.

If a knife is most a knife through cutting, then a body is most a body through hunger.

That night, his thumb hooked in my mouth, I remembered how the raccoon's eyes, without its skull, couldn't shut. I'd like to think, even without ourselves, we could still see. I'd like to think we'd never close.

You and I, we were Americans until we opened our eyes.

//

Truth is none of us has to be beautiful, just warm, like a lived-in house. One where a man walks through all the rooms at night with a baseball bat, smashing out the windows so he can't see the face he makes while he prays.

Truth is the page is a bandage, the words seeping through.

Be still. Can you hear it, the wind driving the river behind the Episcopal church on Wyllis?

The closest I've ever come to god was the silence that filled me after orgasm. In the room of the boy who skinned raccoons, I touched the baseball trophies along his bookshelf the way god touches me, with only my seeing.

Three weeks after Trevor died a trio of tulips in an earthenware pot stopped me in the middle of my mind. I had woken abruptly and, my eyes still glazed from sleep, mistook the dawn light directly hitting the petals for the flowers emitting their own light. I crawled to the glowing cups, thinking I was seeing a miracle, my own burning bush. But when I got closer, my head blocked the rays and the tulips turned off, then on again as I shifted, dazed. This means nothing, I know. But some nothings change everything after them.

After all, we are here only once.

Are you cold? Don't you think it's strange that to be warm is to basically touch the body with the temperature of its marrow?

One of us, tonight, is inside out.

//

This is what I mean when I tell them I grew up in New England. I am not talking about the Patriots or the Red Socks, or autumnal roads flanked by red and gold deciduous trees, or quintessential farm stands offering apple or pumpkin picking to families donning L.L. Bean jackets. I am talking about numbers. I am talking about how lucky you are if the names of your dead do not exceed the fingers on your hands.

How many times have they told you you won't make it here? But not only have you made it here, you make here, you are making.

Once, a soldier on leave from Iraq fucked me so hard I flickered between his arms. I came on and off, like a bulb in a storm. The salt slamming in sparks off our skin. We were both running: two horses, on fire, raising for the river. His knuckles pearl-white around my throat, I blacked in and out of myself, somehow still myself.

What do you do waking up after that? What do you do knowing you had a body that could be killed, even in pleasure, but was spared? I did the first thing that came to mind. I called you, asked what you needed from the store.

A page, turning, is a wing lifted with no twin, and therefore no flight. And yet we are moved.

Hey you, I said one night to myself, *let this body not merely be a point of departure.*

How many mirrors have you tried to prove wrong only to discover, too late, that you were made right?

//

Dear Ma, if you see me wherever you're headed, then I prayed correctly.

Dear Ma, from the wind, I learned a syntax for forwardness, how to move through obstacles by wrapping myself around them. You can make it home this way. Believe me, you can shake the wheat and still be nameless as cokedust on the tender side of a farmboy's fist.

The truth is—to erase us they must burn the page they live on.

In our best light, we *were* the light.

They will want you to succeed, but never more than them. They will write their names on your leash and call you *necessary.*

Horror story: In the back of a car doing 90 on I-85, my veins burning with what I put there, I was a sound changing into its echo.

Can you hear me?

How come each time my hands hurt me, they become more mine?

On a barbed wired fence surrounding an abandoned seaside sanatorium on an overcast day in February, a pink and white dream catcher tangled between the blades.

The truth is there are as many regrets as there are words.

Go past the cemetery on House St. The one with headstones so worn the names look like teeth marks. The oldest grave holds a Mary-Anne Cowder (1784-1784).

In Vietnamese, the word for missing someone and remembering them is the same word: nho. Sometimes, when you ask me over the phone, *Con nho me khong?* I flinch, thinking you meant *Do you remember me?*

Is it wrong that I always miss you more than I remember you?

//

Then, like gravity, like a promise, they will tell you that to be political is to be *merely* angry, and therefore artless, depthless, "raw" and empty. They will speak of the political with embarrassment, as if speaking of Santa Claus or the Easter Bunny. As if to write of one's world and one's life (even something mundane as a bottle of water, under brief examinations: its source and accessibility, how its distributed, protected, sold, is made from political actions) is a rare exception from human life.

They will tell you that superior art is one that "breaks free" from the political, thereby transcending the barriers of difference, uniting people towards "universal truths." They'll say this is achieved through *craft* above all. Let's look at how it's made, they'll say—as if how something is made is alien to the impulse that created it. As if the first chair was hammered into existence without considering the human form.

Because the reward for "well-crafted" erasure is extinction, and often your own.

Because an apolitical life has never existed, will never exist, because we, all of us in the present, are the very sum total of a political history. To say one is apolitical is to say that one has no mother or father, that one has no skeleton.

This does not mean every story, poem, syntactical unit should decry a politics, should pick a side (for even the idea of a side is too narrow), but it should, inside you, be filtered through a gaze which demands *Why and how did I arrive here, in time?*

They will take from your roots and call it discovery. They will call it innovation. But amnesia is not ingenuity.

You know this already.

//

There was that night when, after riding our bikes for two hours so Trevor could score Fentanyl on the outskirts of East Hartford, we sat in the unlit elementary school playground, the swings creaking beneath us. He had just shot up. I watched as he held a flame under the plastic transdermal adhesive, until the Fentanyl bubbled and gathered into a sticky pool at the center. When the plastic started to warp at the edges, browning, he stopped. Then he took the needle and sucked the clear liquid past the black ticks on the cylinder.

Now his sneakers grazed the woodchips that, earlier in the day 4th graders ran through during recess. In the dark the sky-blue hippo, its mouth open where you can crawl through, looked the deep violet of a giant bruise. "Hey, Little Dog?" From his slurred voice, I could tell that his eyes were closed. "Uh huh?" I asked. "Is it, like, true though?" he said. His swing kept creaking, but the woodchips stopped grating his sneakers. "You think you'll really be gay, like, forever? I mean," the swing stopped creaking, "I think I'll be good when I'm 30, you know?"

I couldn't tell if by "really" he meant *very gay or truly gay*, so I said, "Yeah, I'm really gay," not knowing what I meant.

"That's crazy." He laughed, the clipped one you use to test the thickness of a silence.

Then something grazed my mouth. Startled, I clenched my lips around it anyway. Trevor had slipped a bogie in my mouth, and lit it. The flame flashed in his eyes, glazed and blood-shot. I breathed in the sweet scalding smoke, fighting back tears—and succeeding.

//

Round the corner by the traffic light that, at this hour, blinks yellow.

Are you at the bus stop between Harris and Risley yet, where, while walking back from the store with Lan, I was surrounded by a group of neighborhood boys. One of them, whose father, like my father, was also in prison, stepped to my face. Lan looked around, delirious, the plastic bags pulling on her arms.

Say it, the boy demanded. *Come on, bitch. Say it and you and your crazy grandma can go home.* I focused on the boy's voice, how it had pressed on the verge of rage. The other boys repeated the command. They knew the will word marks me as what they need me to be. Because Lan was there, because she was mumbling in Vietnamese and swaying her head, I said it, looking right into their eyes.

"I'm a cocksucker"

"Again, bitch."

"I'm a cocksucker."

The boy stepped back, the others roared from the edge of their shadows. They slapped their knees and doubled over. They came to life.

Later, at home, Lan asked me what they were doing back there. And I lied, said they were playing a game. It was just the scarecrow game, I told her, where you had to stand very still while the boys called you names. It was a test of endurance, I said, smiling.

After making her a peanut butter sandwich, we sat, the TV painting our faces the blue of smudged ink, she turned to me, said, "Don't be a scarecrow anymore, okay, Little Dog?" As she said this she looked at me real serious, her hand, by then smaller than mine, resting on my back, and I swear I almost lost it.

They say the ship is sinking—and yet they keep making cannons instead of lifeboats.

The truth is I'm not well. They got me on Prozac and Ativan, which makes everything so far away. Each morning, I wake up clinging to a piece of driftwood the size of myself.

You asked me what it's like to be a writer and I'm giving you a mess. But it's a mess, Ma—I'm not making this up. I made it down. That's what writing is, after all the nonsense, getting down so low the world offers a merciful new angle, a larger vision made of small things, the lint suddenly a monstrous sheet of fog exactly the size of your eyeball. And you look through it and see the thick steam in the all-night bath house in Flushing, where a hand reached out to me, stopped over the trapped flute of my collarbone. I never saw the face that touch belonged to, but the feeling, the velvet heat of it, was everywhere inside me. Is that not art: to be touched, thinking what we feel is ours—when, in the end, it was another human, in longing, who found us?

If there's a heaven, I don't think I wanna go.

//

The truth is words, abstract as they are, can be solid as cages.

But you don't have to build a cage. You can build a horse.

Let me explain. Once, while driving through a desert in New Mexico, I saw a red stallion rise out of the horizon like something ancient. It grew larger as I drove, its mane touching the mesas punctuating the spines. As I neared, the animal grew nearly 20 ft. in the air, its head darkening my car. Only when I pulled over, approached it by foot, did I see the exhaust pipes running the bridge of its snout, the hubcaps hewn to its flanks, the rusted gears, sheets of reddish metal stripped from the side of eviscerated tractors. Forming the femur was an entire lamppost standing upright, the bulbed glass a joint in the hip socket. It was a sculpture made from pieces of dead machines; a horse written with debris.

Don't let them convince you that writing is only worthy when "elevated" or "heightened." No language is too low, too base when rearranged into the jaw of a beast made of lost things. A writer, if nothing else, is a junkyard artist.

And yet they will give you a cage and tell you to be grateful. They will give you a cage and say it's freedom of speech, that it's always been this way. That this country was built on the cries of truck-loaded hogs on their way to slaughter. But you know better. You will break down the bars and build yourself a horse, a Goliath that does not need to be killed just to prove the worth of small men.

I know. It's not fair that the word *laughter* is trapped inside *slaughter.*

We will have to cut it open, you and I, like a newborn lifted, red and trembling, from the just-shot doe.

Before Houdini made his famous straight jacket escape in the Thames River, his wife, Bess, gave him a long kiss. In doing so, she passed him the key that would save his life.

Keep going down Hubbard. If you forget me, then you've gone too far. Turn back.

//

While cleaning my closet one afternoon I found a Jolly Rancher in the pocket of an old coat. It was from Trevor's truck. He always kept them in his cup holder. I unwrapped it, held it between my fingers. This cube of sugar, I thought, was a witness to the evening Trevor and I parked in the liquor store lot singing off key and telling jokes. The memory of our laughter is inside it. "Tell me what you know," I whispered, turning it so that it caught the light from the window. Then I walked inside the closest, closed the door, sat down in the tight dark, and placed the candy, gently and cool, in my mouth. Green Apple.

I'm writing fast as I can. Can you feel it?

I'm not with you because I'm at war with everything but you.

Is the red wool scarf I got you warm enough?

To be loved well is a rare thing; to love well even rarer. But you know this already.

If you're reading this, and you're in the next life, and you're a girl named Rose (again) with a childhood not cut short by war. If you're under your covers on a raised bed in a lamp-lit room surrounded by your favorite books, maybe you'll recognize us, here, in your hands.

Yes, there's such a thing as useful sadness, like brushing your teeth in a motel bathroom as an adult imagining your parents are curled on the bed, watching TV on an American vacation you never took.

This way, you brush a little longer. You get a little cleaner.

A body beside a body inside a life. That's called parataxis. That's called the future.

We're almost there.

Head around the bend, past the second stop sign with the word "H8" spray-painted in white on the bottom. Walk toward the grey house, the one with its left side darker from exhaust blown from the scrapyard's furnace across the highway.

There's the upstairs window where, one night long ago, I woke to a blizzard, the street below like one inside a snow globe. I was five or six and didn't know things ended. I thought the snow would continue to the sky's brim—then beyond, touching god's fingertips as he dozed in his reading chair, the equations scattered across the floor of his study. That by morning we would all be sealed inside a blue-white stillness and no one would be taken to heaven. No one would have to leave.

It is said, and I believe it, that even the person you bump into on the street is the one you've met in your past life.

What were we before we were we? We must've been standing by the shoulder of a dirt road while the city burned. We must've been disappearing, like we are now. I felt nothing but knew I was alive because I could still see your face through the smoke. My eyes worked to keep you inside my head, my little world. That seeing, it was my truest act of hunger.

Green Apple.

Like snow covering the particulars of the city, they will say we never happened, that our survival was a myth. But they're wrong. You and I, we were real. We laughed knowing joy would tear the stitches from our lips.

Remember, the rules, like streets, can only take you to *known* places. Underneath the grid is a field—it was always there—where to be lost is never to be wrong, but simply more.

As a rule, be more.

As a rule, "little" is always smaller than "small." Don't ask me why.

I'm sorry I don't call enough.

Green Apple.

I know this is only paper—but take my hand. Things here are often elsewhere.

I'm sorry I keep saying *How are you?* when I really mean *Are you happy?*

Hey, if you find yourself trapped inside a dimming world, remember it was always this dark inside the body. Where the heart, like any law, beats for no reason but its memory of breaking.

Hey. If you find yourself, then your hands are yours to keep.

Good luck.

Goodnight.

Goodbye.

Good lord, Green Apple.

ON WRITING FROM UNINCORPORATED TERRITORY

Craig Santos Perez

Introduction

Stories are an important part of my indigenous Chamorro culture. Stories are ocean-going vessels that carry our memories, customs, ethics, histories, politics, fears, hopes, and dreams. Stories teach us where we come from in order to better understand the present and to navigate the future. Growing up on Guam, I was surrounded by stories. My parents, grandparents, aunties and uncles loved talking stories around the dining table, the barbecue grill, the beach, or after church. I always loved hearing my relatives talk-story and listening to their voices interweave.

I did not start writing poetry seriously until my family migrated to California when I was 15 years old. I attended a public high school and was fortunate to have very inspiring English teachers who taught a multicultural selection of literature. Poetry became a way for me to stay connected to my homeland and to express the traumas of migration. I continued writing as an undergraduate student at the University of Redlands in Southern California, where I majored in interdisciplinary studies. I focused on courses in literature, creative writing, and art history. I studied with poets Joy Manesiotis and Ralph Angel, and the literary scholars Bill McDonald and Daniel Kiefer. My senior projects included essays on the Russian novelist Dostoevsky and the Italian renaissance painter, Tintoretto; a creative writing portfolio; an exhibit of my environmental photography; and a series of large scale multimedia paintings. In all these projects, I focused on the relationship between ethics and aesthetics, a relationship I would continue to explore when I attended the University of San Francisco for my MFA. I studied multicultural and international poetry and poetics with Aaron Shurin, Rusty Morrison, Truong Tran, Rob Halpern, D.A. Powell, Paul Hoover, and Susan Gevirtz. My MFA thesis would later become my first book of poems.

After I completed the MFA, I attended the Ph.D. program in Comparative Ethnic Studies at the University of California, Berkeley. While my coursework focused on ethnic studies and critical race theory, I was fortunate to study with many literary scholars who approached literature through an ethnic studies lens. For example, I studied Latinx literature and theory with Jose David Saldivar, Asian American Literature and Theory with Sau-Ling Wong, and Native American Literature and Theory with Beth Piatote and Hertha Sweet Wong. As part of my doctoral area exams, I independently studied Pacific Islander Literature and Theory, and my dissertation focused on expressions of indigenous identity in contemporary Chamorro literature. And even though I was not in the English department, I had the opportunity to meet and engage with several of their renowned faculty, including Lyn Hejinian, C.S. Giscombe, Robert Hass, and Alfred Arteaga.

I share my educational biography because it has shaped my practice, pedagogy, and beliefs in poetry and poetics. My teachers have taught me the importance of stories in all cultures and across histories and national borders. I have studied and have been mentored by writers and scholars from different ethnic groups, and I have learned how stories can inspire and empower people, especially people who have experienced oppression, slavery, genocide, migration, and other injustices. I also learned how stories can mobilize human rights, civil rights, environmental rights, animal rights, and indigenous rights movements. This connection has also led me to become involved with decolonial, demilitarization, and environmental justice activism. All of this has helped me tell my own story of my family, culture, and homeland.

For the past ten years, I have been working on a series of books titled *from unincorporated territory*. Thus far, four volumes have been completed, each with its own name in Chamorro: *from unincorporated territory [hacha]* (2008), *from unincorporated territory [saina]* (2010), *from unincorporated territory [guma']* (2014), and *from unincorporated territory [lukao]* (2017). These books (totaling around 350 pages) attempt to articulate Guam's history and politics, as well as the culture and memories of Chamorros at home and abroad. The poems are written in an experimental form that is modeled on frameworks from Pacific, indigenous, postcolonial, hybrid, documentary, and ecological poetics.

For the remainder of this essay, I will discuss my poetics in more detail and will end with a bibliography of scholarship that has been written about my work. Hopefully there will be something of interest to both writers and scholars.

Poetics

1. Write from:

From indicates a particular time or place as a starting point; from refers to a specific location as the first of two limits; from imagines a cause, an agent, an instrument, a source, or an origin; from marks separation, removal, or exclusion; from differentiates borders. "Where are you from?" In the preface to my first book of poems, I wrote: "On some maps, Guam doesn't exist; I point to an empty space in the Pacific and say, 'I'm from here.' On some maps, Guam is a small, unnamed island; I say, 'I'm from this unnamed place.' On some maps, Guam is named 'Guam, USA.' I say, 'I'm from a territory of the United States.'"

from excerptus: "pluck out" from ex- "out" + carpere "gather" or "harvest"

From also indicates an excerpt or a passage quoted from a source. My own passage and migration from Guam to California often feels like living an excerpted existence; while my body lives here, my heart still lives in my homeland. Poetry is a way for me to bring together these excerpted spaces via the transient, processional, and migratory cartographies of the page. Each of my poems, and each of my books, and seemingly every breath I take, carries the from and bears its weight and incompleteness.

2. Write Oceanic

The imagination is an ocean of possibilities. I imagine the blank page as an excerpt of the ocean. The ocean is storied and heavy with history, myth, rumor, genealogy, loss, war, money, the dead, life, and even plastic. The ocean is not "aqua nullius." The page, then, is never truly blank. The page consists of submerged volcanoes of story and unfathomable depths of meaning.

Each word is an island. The visible part of the word is its textual body; the invisible part of the word is the submerged mountain of meaning. Words emerging from the silence are islands forming. No word is just an island, every word is part of a sentence, an archipelago. The space between is defined by referential waves and currents.

Oceanic stories are vessels for cultural beliefs, values, customs, histories, genealogies, politics, and memories. Stories weave generations and geographies. Stories protest and mourn the ravages of colonialism, articulate and promote cultural revitalization, and imagine and express decolonization.

3. Write Archipelagic

An individual book is an island with a unique linguistic geography and ecology, as well as a unique poetic landscape and seascape. The book-island is inhabited by the living and the dead, the human and the non-human, multiple voices and silences. The book-island vibrates with the complexity of the present moment and the depths of history and genealogy, culture and politics, scars and bone and blood.

A book series is an archipelago, a birthing and formation of book-islands. Like an archipelago, the books in an ongoing series are related and woven to the other islands, yet unique and different. Reading the books in a series is akin to traveling and listening across the archipelago.

Because Guam is part of an archipelago, the geography inspired the form of my *from unincorporated territory* book series. Additionally, the unfolding nature of memory, learning, listening, sharing, and storytelling informed the serial nature of the work. To me, the complexity of the story of Guam and the Chamorro people — entangled in the complications of ongoing colonialism and militarism — inspired the ongoing serial form.

The first book of the series, *from unincorporated territory [hacha]* (2008), focused on my grandfather's life and experience on Guam when the island was occupied by Japan's military during World War II. The second book, *from unincorporated territory [saina]* (2010), focused on my grandmother's contrasting experience during that same period. The third book, *from unincorporated territory [guma']* (2014), echoes and enlarges the earlier books through the themes of family, militarization, cultural identity, migration and colonialism. Furthermore, *[guma']* focuses on my own return to my home island after living away (in California) for 15 years. I explore how the island has changed and how my idea of home has changed. I also meditate upon the memories that I have carried with me, as well as all that I have forgotten and left behind.

The titles are meant to mark and name different books in the same series. Just as an archipelago has a name, such as the Marianas Archipelago, each island of the archipelago has its own unique name. The names can be translated as [one], [elder], and [home]. My first book was given the name [hacha], to mark it as the first book, first island, first voice. While one might expect the second book to be named, second, I chose the name, [elder], to resist that linearity and instead highlight genealogy, or the past. The third book, which means house or home, was an attempt to weave together time and space (the house or book as spatial and temporal). The fourth book, *from unincorporated territory [lukao]* (2017), includes themes of birth, creation, parenthood, money, climate colonialism, militarization, migration, and extinction. The Chamorro name of the book, [lukao], means procession.

My multi-book project also formed through my study of the "long poem:" Pound's Cantos, Williams' Paterson, H.D.'s Trilogy, Zukofsky's "A," and Olson's Maximus. I loved how these books were able to attain a breadth and depth of vision and voice. One difference between my project and other "long poems" is that my long poem will always contain the "from," always eluding the closure of completion.

I also became intrigued by how certain poets write trans-book poems: such as Duncan's "Passages" and Mackey's "Songs of the Andoumboulou." I employ this kind of trans-book threading in my own work as poems change and continue across books (for example, excerpts from the poems "from tidelands" and "from aerial roots" appear in both my first and second books). These threaded poems differ from Duncan and Mackey's work because I resist the linearity of numbering that their work employs.

4. Write Cartographic

I use diagrams, maps, illustrations, collage visual poetry as a way to foreground the relationship between storytelling, mapping, and navigation. Just as maps have used illustrations (sometimes visual, sometimes typographical), I believe poetry can both enhance and disrupt our visual literacy.

One incessant typographical presence throughout my work is the tilde (~). Besides resembling an ocean current and containing the word "tide" in its body, the tilde has many intriguing uses. In languages, the tilde is used to indicate a change of pronunciation. As you know, I use many different kinds of discourse in my work (historical, political, personal, etc.) and the tilde is meant to indicate a shift in the discursive poetic frame. In mathematics, the tilde is used to show equivalence (i.e. x~y). Throughout my work, I want to show that personal or familial narratives have an equivalent importance to official historical and political discourses.

Cartographic representations of the Pacific Ocean developed in Europe at the end of the 15th century, when the Americas were incorporated into maps: the Pacific became a wide empty space separating Asia and America. In European world maps, Europe is placed at the center and "Oceania" is divided into two opposite halves on the margins. As imperialism progressed, every new voyage incorporated new data into new maps.

As I mention in the preface to my first book, the invisibility of Guam on many maps—whether actual maps or the maps of history—has always haunted me. One hope for my poetry is to enact an emerging map of "Guam" both as a place and as a signifier.

The "actual maps" in my first book are, to me, both visual poems and illustrations of the rest of the work. In my imagination, they function in two ways: first, they center "Guam," a locating signifier often omitted from many maps. Second, the maps are meant to provide a counterpoint to the actual stories that are told throughout the book. While maps can locate, chart, and represent (and through this representation tell an abstracted story), they never show us the human voices of a place. I place this abstract, aerial view of "Guam" alongside the more embodied and rooted portraits of place and people.

"Song maps" refer to the songs, chants, and oral stories that were created to help seafarers navigate oceanic and archipelagic spaces. Pacific navigational techniques are often understood as a "visual literacy," in the sense that a navigator has to be able to "read" the natural world in order to make safe landfall. The key features include reading the stars, ocean efflorescence, wave currents, and fish and bird migrations.

Scholars and navigators describe this technique as "moving islands" because in these songs, the canoe is conceptualized as remaining still, while the stars, islands, birds, fish, and waves all move in concert. Islands not only move, but islands also expand and contract. For example, if you see an offshore bird associated with a certain island, then you know that island is nearby (thus, it has figuratively, expanded).

With this in mind, I imagine that poems are song maps of my own journey to find Guam across historical and diasporic distances. I imagine the reader is in a still canoe, reading the songs in order to navigate the archipelago of memory and story. In this way, books and words become moving islands, expanding and contracting, inhaling and exhaling.

Notes

Baxter, Katherine and Lytton Smith. "Writing in Translation: Robert Sullivan's Star Waka and Craig Santos Perez's from unincorporated territory." Literary Geographies (2.2) (2016): 263-283.
Bevacqua, Michael Lujan. "The Song Maps of Craig Santos Perez." Transmotion 1.1 (2015).
Briggs, Robert J. "There's no place (Like Home): Craig Santos Perez's poetry as military strategy." Green Letters: Studies in Ecocriticism (2016).

Clark, Ryan. The Appositional Project: Craig Santos Perez's from unincorporated territory [saina]. Spoon River Poetry Review (2013).
Cocola, Jim. "Forget your Pastoral: Haunani-Kay Trask and Craig Santos Perez," chapter in Places in the Making: Cultural Geography in American Poetry (University of Iowa Press, 2016)
Dick, Jennifer K. "Craig Santos Perez and Myung Mi Kim: Voicing the Integral Divide: Transcending Suffering by Reshaping American History and Language," in American Multiculturalism in Context: Views from at Home and Abroad, edited by Sami Ludwig (Cambridge Scholars Publishing, 2017): 203-220.
Heim, Otto. "Locating Guam: The Cartography of the Pacific and Craig Santos Perez's Re-mapping of Unincorporated Territory." In New Directions in Travel Studies (Palgrave 2015).
Hsu, Hsuan. "Guahan (Guam), Literary Emergence, and the American Pacific in Homebase and from unincorporated territory." *American Literary History* (Summer 2012) 24: 2.
Lai, Paul. "Discontiguous States of America: The Paradox of Unincorporation in Craig Santos Perez's Poetics of Chamorro Guam." *The Journal of Transnational American Studies*, Volume 3, Issue 2, 2011.
Schlund-Vials, Cathy J. „'Finding' Guam: Distant Epistemologies and Cartographic Pedagogies." *Asian American Literature: Discourses and Pedagogies 5* (2014): 45-60.
Woodward, Valerie. "I Guess They Didn't Want Us Asking Too Many Questions": Reading American Empire in Guam." The Contemporary Pacific, Volume 25, Number 1, Spring 2013: 67-91.

THE MONSTROSITY:
NOTES TOWARDS A FRANKENPO

Kenji C. Liu

I.

Growing up immersed in Japanese intransitive verbs, I learn to omit the subject in a sentence. Later as an adult and a poet, I begin to negate the American English insistence on explicit subject-verb pairs. Or rather, active negation of the active voice begins. Why should a voice be labeled and gendered as "passive" as if it does nothing? It does much more than it seems: the receiver has to perceive meanings through context. It leaves room for the relationship between the communicators. Or rather, room is left for the meaning to be supplied through relationship.

This is how Godzilla would speak, despite appearances.

II.

> *His eyes are staring, his mouth is open, his wings are spread. This is how one pictures the angel of history. His face is turned toward the past. Where we perceive a chain of events, he sees one single catastrophe which keeps piling wreckage upon wreckage and hurls it in front of his feet. The angel would like to stay, awaken the dead, and make whole what has been smashed. But a storm is blowing from Paradise; it has got caught in his wings with such violence that the angel can no longer close them. This storm irresistibly propels him into the future to which his back is turned, while the pile of debris before him grows skyward. This storm is what we call progress.*
>
> Walter Benjamin on Paul Klee's monoprint, "Angelus Novus," in *Theses on the Philosophy of History* (1940).

Paul Klee's "Angelus Novus" is a rogue taxidermy, an anatomically reversed griffin. A wild mane whips around the lion-like face, uneven teeth frame an expression of surprise, eyes slightly askew. The angel's wings are also hands, recalling a feathered, avian dinosaur, and bird-like legs dangle under a set of tail feathers. This is a "new angel," which for Walter Benjamin, living with and between two world wars, comes to represent the emptiness and horror present in the discursive and material realities of modernity. A witness to the wreckage of modernity, the angel is itself patched together from different beasts. A monstrous presence is needed to respond to monstrous times.

We see this reflected in different poets: Don Mee Choi, Bhanu Kapil, Barbara Jane Reyes, Joyelle McSweeney, Kim Hyesoon, Hiromi Ito, Raul Zurita, and Dolores Dorantes. These are the writers whose work I am most familiar with. Because of centuries of capitalist extremism—colonialism, imperialism, and neoliberalism—damning evidence has piled up. The logic of Progress, the pernicious idea that all of humanity and history always advances towards better conditions under Western guidance, is no logic at all. It is a dissipating magic spell. It has failed because its pretense of universality is just a pretense. The Universal only benefits a few. With right-wing nationalist and neo-fascist populists sweeping to power in the US and Europe exploiting the cracks in neoliberal capitalism, the wreckage is more evident to both the left and right. It is our response that differs, our political commitment to and solidarity with the historic margins.

III.

I am no doubt not the only one who writes in order to have no face. Do not ask who I am and do not ask me to remain the same: leave it to our bureaucrats and our police to see that our papers are in order. At least spare us their morality when we write.

Michel Foucault, *The Archaeology of Knowledge*

Reading Foucault, I cultivate a suspicion of the master narrative and the all-knowing author in its many forms. For the arrogance of the one who Knows, for the expert whose expertise is universal and marginalizes any alternatives. For the white male explorer whose perspective is unquestionable, unassailable because supposedly neutral, objective, and universal. In response, drawing on Japanese grammar, I experiment with minimizing the western, hyper-individuated, confessional self—not to efface the hand that writes, but to contextualize it in all that produces it as a cultural point of view. The subject is not solid, but a construction—of history, race, class, gender, religion, and more.

IV.

There are compatible concepts in Buddhism. For instance, practicing vipassana meditation for many years and experiencing direct glimpses of the changing, contingent nature of self. In the Satipatthana Sutta, there are instructions for a meditation on the body in its physical details, on its organs, fluids, systems, and fibers, each part isolated and reflected on separately. By contemplating each part, equanimity is cultivated and attachment to the body as me or mine is weakened. Through active practice, it becomes possible to loosen the grip on conventional identity, to regard it as a temporary vessel. And yet the conventional self is constantly produced through interaction with its environment. In socially engaged Buddhism, the significance of self, community, and identity is not minimized, because they influence and are influenced by our economic, cultural, and political experiences. There are also ethical precepts, guidelines for cultivating the conditions for happiness and ending suffering, which focuses the gaze back into the world. Holding one's communities and commitments in a field of compassion, a gentle titration ensues between self and un- or re-making the self. This is a poetic practice of self that embraces more than one simultaneous reality, but never ignores the world.

V.

The angelic, floating white woman in John Gast's 1872 painting "American Progress" is a celebration of the colonization of North America, and she is also a monster. An eroticized symbol of an expansionist, selectively benevolent state, beneath the exterior she is Frankenstein's monstrosity, patched together from genocide, slavery, capitalist exploitation, and racialized, gendered violence, blown westward by the force of their explosions. The rest of us, the majority, are either not in this painting or pushed to its edges, buried under its pastoral. Yet in the wreckage we find ways to recycle, compost, to be a worm in the gut of the state. We awaken the dead. Benjamin's angel cannot see the future with its back turned to it, but we create from what is in front of us, and that is a kind of future. It exists not in order to produce use-value, but to create beauty, an effort to resist monetization.

VI.

Gazing back at the wreckage as I am swept towards the future, my family strides onto the path. My grandmother's Japan was/is an imperial power. Buddhism as a tool of domination. By letting go of self in service of a "compassionate" war, the monk-soldier becomes a single-minded, efficient killer. Ideology: to expand the Japanese Empire in order to prevent Europe from conquering Asia. There is the Japanese occupation of my grandfather's Taiwan, 1895-1945. Atomic obliteration in the Pacific, in Japan. The awakening of Godzilla. This too is wreckage, with its long half-life.

VII.

And then, how does one reckon with Confucianism? I consult the online I Ching divination system, digital representative of ancient Chinese heteropatriarchy, rectifier of proper, harmonious social relations. Interviewing the online I Ching (which is itself a British translation), asking it questions it can never really answer, that in a way, are against its own best interest. Dear I Ching, what is the best way to end patriarchy? What is the best way to end white supremacy? Divine your own destruction. Inserting its answers into Google Translate, going through the languages of my family—from English to Traditional Chinese to Japanese and back to English—imitates migration. If Hakka was available this would be included, too. The I Ching's voice is forced to mutate, receding in some places, exploding in others. The imperfection of translation, the impossibility of one-to-one correspondence of meaning, results in the intentional production of wreckage. Like an n+7 tower of babel. Cutting up the results, hunting among the trash for useful pieces with which to build new, imperfect responses.

VIII.

I was going to create a new kind of man. This man would love me more than a son loves his father. I also thought that if I could make lifeless parts live, maybe I could bring the dead back to life.
From *Frankenstein* (abridged), by Mary Shelley

To choose and collect bodies, to dissect, disaggregate, and randomize parts. To rearrange and merge, to erase the extraneous, to sew together. To reanimate. For Dr. Frankenstein, this work begins as a kind of progress, an invention of science with tremendous potential for human benefit. It ends in tragedy, and a monster is left to roam the world. Since the European Enlightenment, the language of universal "progress" has justified colonial and imperial violences both overt and subtle. It is both "manifest destiny" and the "white man's burden" to spread North American and European disasters everywhere. Aimé Césaire notes in *Discourse on Colonialism* that colonial Europe, whose ostensible reason for being is benevolence while its actual motive is exploitation, is "indefensible." It has left a trail of lifeless parts in the name of the father. But we can also find creativity in the middle of trash: we find new relationships between the parts.

Mutations, reanimations of texts. Digging up bodies, text bodies with antagonistic relations, mutually generative relations, or seemingly no relationship at all. Isolating every word, randomizing order, mixing. Using text manipulation software, moving body parts, organs, systems, from one location to another. Chopping, erasing, sewing. Searching for new connections, unseen formations. Building new bodies because the old ones are indefensible. Or composting—bodies growing out of the indefensibility of the old.

Not an attempt to create a new kind of man, but to grow a monster of compassion and ferocity. Because capitalism, white supremacy, heteropatriarchy is so monstrous, perhaps only a Godzilla can counter it. Systems of dehumanization proliferate, isolate and pathologize communities that deviate from the norm. In solidarity with Godzilla—child of the atomic bomb—we can commit rogue taxidermy against its texts—a Frankenstein poetry, a frankenpo. Perhaps only monsters can reinvent humanity, though not with a replacement humanism or dominant universal. Instead, something only monsters, having experienced destruction, can imagine—an ethics of mutual grieving, radical generosity, hospitality. A feral, generous poetry arriving from the future we are always being blown into.

IX.

Isolate the 45th US President's inauguration speech, noted by the *Washington Post* for being uniquely apocalyptic in the history of such speeches. Then dig up the speech given by Senator Palpatine to the Galactic Senate in *Star Wars III: Revenge of the Sith*, in which Palpatine revokes democracy and becomes the Emperor. Isolate words, mixing and randomizing. Search for unique juxtapositions, odd phrases and images. See what connections and contradictions emerge or get amplified.

Find a feminist article discussing the US mainstream emasculation of Asian American men. Mix it with the complete English subtitles from Wong Kar-Wai's sexy Hong Kong masterpiece, *In the Mood for Love*. Or mix an article on Japanese "genderless danshi" with a Buddhist sutta on loving-kindness, and the screenplay of the animated film, *The Last Unicorn*. Through this process, affirm multiple sexualities and gender expressions.

Steal text from an 1845 article in which the phrase "manifest destiny" is first used, justifying the annexation of Texas from Mexico. Mix it with itself. Fuck it up. What hidden messages emerge? How can the text be used to implicate itself?

What indefensible monstrosities do we come from, live in? What new bodies do we need in order to survive and live? What texts can we conjure from the wreck, whose ferocious griffin hospitality can we inhabit? Can we awaken the dead?

X.

A monstrous poetry,[1] troubling the text. The world as text. Kaiju/Godzilla poetry. Mutant poetry. Cyborg poetry.[2] Feral,[3] necropastoral[4] poetry. Undocumented poetry. Taxidermy poetry.[5] Witch/brujx poetry.[6] Cunt-up poetry.[7] Compost poetry. Literary rasquachismo.[8] A trash aesthetic.[9] Poetry with little use for the shiny, never-quite-fulfilled or fulfilling promises of modernity, nationalisms, neoliberalism. Cross-translating between worlds, between English and Englishes, between the past, now, and what might come. Not translating for clarity or legibility, but to point out gaps and the power relations that create them.[10] Composting the master narrative and growing new bodies, new abilities. Diving into the wreckage.[11] We need poetry that already knew it was political, and didn't have to be convinced.

What is the subject being produced through frankenpo? One who makes and remakes, exactly because destruction has never been complete. There are always parts leftover. Though intersectional and inseparable from the wreck, we also become ferociously different—imperfect, wild, succulent. A monstrously generous poetry, in a world of inhuman monstrosity.

With thanks to Vickie Vértiz and Heidi Andrea Rhodes for their generative readings and interventions. There are many more poets whose work could be noted here.

Notes

1. Sor Juana Inés de la Cruz (https://bostonreview.net/literature-culture-poetry/joyelle-mcsweeney-monstrosity-sor-juana)
2. Margaret Rhee
3. Bhanu Kapil
4. Joyelle McSweeney
5. Rajiv Mohabir
6. Angel Dominguez
7. Dodie Bellamy
8. Amalia Mesa-Baines and Tomás Ybarra-Frausto
9. Ben Highmore
10. Jen Hofer
11. Adrienne Rich

ABOUT THIS BOOK

About the Editors

Amanda Galvan Huynh is the author of a chapbook, *Songs of Brujería* (Big Lucks, 2019). She has received fellowships from The MacDowell Colony, the Sewanee Writers' Conference, Sundress Academy for the Arts, Vermont Studio Center, NY Summer Writers Institute, and Robert Rauschenberg Foundation. She is a winner of a 2016 AWP Intro Journal Project Award, and a finalist for the 2017 Poetry Society of America Chapbook Fellowship. www.amandagalvanhuynh.com

Luisa A. Igloria is the winner of the 2015 Resurgence Prize (UK), the world's first major award for ecopoetry, selected by former UK poet laureate Sir Andrew Motion, Alice Oswald, and Jo Shapcott. Former US Poet Laureate Natasha Trethewey selected her chapbook *What is Left of Wings, I Ask* as the 2018 recipient of the Center for the Book Arts Letterpress Poetry Chapbook award. Other works include *The Buddha Wonders if She is Having a Mid-Life Crisis* (Phoenicia Publishing, Montreal, 2018), *Ode to the Heart Smaller than a Pencil Eraser* (2014 May Swenson Prize, Utah State University Press), and 12 other books. She teaches on the faculty of the MFA Creative Writing Program at Old Dominion University, which she directed from 2009-2015. Her website is: www.luisaigloria.com

About the Authors

Ernesto L. Abeytia is a Spanish-American poet. He holds an MFA from Arizona State University and MAs from Saint Louis University and the Autonomous University of Madrid. His poems have appeared or are forthcoming in *Crab Orchard Review, Fugue, Glass Poetry, PBS NewsHour, The Shallow Ends, Zócalo Public Square*, and elsewhere. He teaches at Arizona State University. You can follow him on Twitter: @eabeytia.

Dr. Melissa Coss Aquino, is a Puerto Rican writer from The Bronx and an Associate Professor in the English department at Bronx Community College, CUNY. She serves as the co-faculty advisor for *Thesis*, the literary journal of BCC. Her work has been published in *Callaloo, The Fairy Tale Review, Hippocampus* and *Centro*. Her book, *Jesús Colón: 100 Years of A Radical Puerto Rican in New York* is under contract and set to be published in 2019. She received her MFA from The City College of New York, CUNY and her Ph.D. from The Graduate Center, CUNY in English. She is a proud VONA, AROHO and Hedgebrook alumna.

José Angel Araguz is a CantoMundo fellow and the author of seven chapbooks as well as the collections *Everything We Think We Hear, Small Fires*, and *Until We Are Level Again*. His poems, prose, and reviews have appeared in *Crab Creek Review, Prairie Schooner, The Windward Review*, and *The Bind*. He serves as an editor for the journal *Right Hand Pointing* and is on the editing staff of Airlie Press. A recent finalist for the Oregon Book Award, he runs the poetry blog *The Friday Influence* and teaches English and creative writing at Linfield College.

Remica L. Bingham-Risher, a native of Phoenix, Arizona, is a Cave Canem fellow and Affrilachian Poet. Among other journals, her work has been published in *The New York Times, The Writer's Chronicle, Callaloo* and *Essence*. She is the author of *Conversion* (Lotus, 2006) winner of the Naomi Long Madgett Poetry Award, *What We Ask of Flesh* (Etruscan, 2013) shortlisted for the Hurston/Wright Legacy Award and *Starlight & Error* (Diode, 2017) winner of the Diode Editions Book Award and a finalist for the Library of Virginia Book Award. She is the Director of Quality Enhancement Plan Initiatives at Old Dominion University. She resides in Norfolk, VA with her husband and children.

Ching-In Chen is the author of *The Heart's Traffic* (Arktoi Books), *recombinant* (Kelsey Street Press) and *to make black paper sing* (speCt! books). They are co-editor of *The Revolution Starts at Home: Confronting Intimate Violence Within Activist Communities* (South End Press; AK Press) and *Here is a Pen: An Anthology of West Coast Kundiman Poets* (Achiote Press). A Kundiman, Lambda, Watering Hole and Callaloo Fellow, they are part of the Macondo and Voices of Our Nations Arts Foundation writing communities. Their work has appeared in *The Best American Experimental Writing*, *The &NOW Awards 3: The Best Innovative Writing*, and *Troubling the Line: Trans and Genderqueer Poetry and Poetics*. They serve as poetry editor of the *Texas Review*. www.chinginchen.com

Wendy A. Gaudin is an American historian, an essayist, a poet, and a university educator. She is the descendant of Louisiana Creoles who migrated to California. Her essays explore Creole history and narrative, her family's history in Louisiana and New Orleans, and her experience traveling and living as a mixed race person in Vietnam. Her most recent publications appear in *Puerto del Sol*, the *Rappahannock Review*, the *Indiana Review*, the *New Orleans Review*, and *About Place Journal*. Her essay, "Beauty," was awarded the 2016 Torch Memorial Prize for Creative Nonfiction from the North American Review.

Abigail Licad is a 1.5-generation Filipino American who immigrated to the U.S. with her family at age 13. She received her B.A. from University of California-Berkeley and her M.Phil in literature from Oxford University. Her work has been published in *Calyx, Smartish Pace, San Francisco Chronicle*, and *Los Angeles Times*, among others. She has served as a Rotary International Ambassadorial Scholar to Senegal and as *Hyphen* magazine's editor in chief. She lives and works in the San Francisco Bay Area.

Kenji C. Liu is author of *Monsters I Have Been* (2019, Alice James Books) and *Map of an Onion*, national winner of the 2015 Hillary Gravendyk Poetry Prize (Inlandia Institute). His poetry is in *American Poetry Review, Action Yes!, Anomaly*, Split This Rock's poem of the week series, several anthologies, and two chapbooks, *Craters: A Field Guide* (2017) and *You Left Without Your Shoes* (2009). A Kundiman fellow and an alumnus of VONA/Voices, the Djerassi Resident Artist Program, and the Community of Writers, he lives in Los Angeles. @kenjicliu

Born in Manila, Philippines and raised in the U.S. and Saudi Arabia, **Sasha Pimentel** is the author of *For Want of Water: and other poems* (Beacon Press, 2017), selected by Gregory Pardlo as a winner of the 2016 National Poetry Series. *For Want of Water* is also winner of the 2017 Helen C. Smith Memorial Award and was longlisted for the 2018 PEN/Open Book Award. Her poems and essays have recently appeared in *The New York Times Sunday Magazine, PBS News Hour, The American Poetry Review, New England Review, Guernica, Lit Hub, Poets & Writers* and *poets.org*. She's also the author of I*nsides She Swallowed* (West End Press, 2010), winner of the 2011 American Book Award. She's an Associate Professor of poetry and creative nonfiction in a bilingual (Spanish-English) MFA Program to students from across the Americas at the University of Texas at El Paso, on the border of Ciudad Juárez, México, and winner of the University of Texas system's 2015 Board of Regents' Outstanding Teaching Award. She will be the holder of the Picador Guest Professorship for Literature at Leipzig University, Germany for the winter 2018-2019 term.

Khadijah Queen is the author of five books of poetry and hybrid prose, most recently I*>m So Fine: A List of Famous Men & What I Had On* (YesYes Books 2017). Her verse play, *Non-Sequitur* (Litmus Press 2015), won the Leslie Scalapino Award for Innovative Women Performance Writers, produced by The Relationship theater company in December 2015 at Theaterlab in New York City. Individual works appear in *Fence, Poetry, Tin House, American Poetry Review, Best American Non-Required Reading* and widely elsewhere. She is an assistant professor of creative writing at University of Colorado, Boulder, and serves as core faculty for the Mile-High MFA program at Regis University.

Tony Robles—"The People's Poet of San Francisco" and author of two books of poems and short stories, *Cool Don't Live Here No More—A Letter to San Francisco*, and *Fingerprints of a Hunger Strike*. Was a short list finalist for poet laureate of San Francisco in 2017 and awarded the San Francisco Art Commission literary grant the same year. Was nominated for the Pushcart Prize for his short story, "In My Country" in 2010. Works as a tenant advocate in San Francisco.

Dr. Craig Santos Perez is a native Chamorro poet from the Pacific Island of Guam. He is the co-editor of three anthologies and the author of four books of poetry. He holds an MFA in Creative Writing from the University of San Francisco and a Ph.D. in Ethnic Studies from the University of California, Berkeley. He is an Associate Professor in the English Department at the University of Hawai'i, Mānoa.

Tim Seibles is the author of several poetry collections including *Hurdy-Gurdy, Hammerlock, Buffalo Head Solos,* and *Fast Animal,* which was a finalist for the 2012 National Book Award. In 2013 he won both the Pen Oakland Josephine Miles Award for poetry and the Theodore Roethke Memorial Poetry Prize. His latest collection, *One Turn Around the Sun,* was released in 2017. Tim is the current Poet Laureate of Virginia and is a Professor of English at Old Dominion University where he teaches literature as well as classes in the MFA in writing program.

Addie Tsai teaches courses in literature, creative writing, and humanities at Houston Community College. She collaborated with Dominic Walsh Dance Theater on *Victor Frankenstein* and *Camille Claudel,* among others. Addie holds an MFA from Warren Wilson College and a doctorate in Dance from Texas Woman's University. Her queer Asian young adult novel, *Dear Twin,* is forthcoming from Metonymy Press. Her writing has been published in *Banango Street, The Offing, The Collagist, The Feminist Wire,* and elsewhere. She is the Nonfiction Editor at *The Grief Diaries,* and Senior Associate Editor in Poetry at *The Flexible Persona.*

Mai Der Vang is the author of *Afterland* (Graywolf Press, 2017), winner of the 2016 Walt Whitman Award of the Academy of American Poets, longlisted for the 2017 National Book Award in Poetry, and a finalist for the 2018 Kate Tufts Discovery Award. The recipient of a Lannan Literary Fellowship, she served as a Visiting Writer at the School of the Art Institute of Chicago. Her poetry has appeared or is forthcoming in *Poetry, Tin House,* and *the American Poetry Review,* among other journals and anthologies. Her essays have been published in the *New York Times, the Washington Post*, and elsewhere. Mai Der is a member of the Hmong American Writers' Circle where she co-edited *How Do I Begin: A Hmong American Literary Anthology*. A Kundiman fellow, Mai Der has completed residencies at Civitella Ranieri and Hedgebrook. Born and raised in Fresno, California, she earned degrees from the University of California Berkeley and Columbia University. Commencing Fall 2019, Mai Der will join the Creative Writing MFA faculty at Fresno State as an Assistant Professor of English in Creative Writing.

Poet and essayist **Ocean Vuong** is the author of the best-selling, *Night Sky with Exit Wounds*. A New York Times Top 10 Book of 2016, the debut was a winner of the Whiting Award, the Thom Gunn Award, and the Forward Prize for Best First Collection, and was a finalist for the T.S. Eliot Prize, the Kate Tufts Discovery Award and the Lambda Literary Award. A Ruth Lilly fellow from the Poetry Foundation, his honors include fellowships from the Lannan Foundation, the Civitella Ranieri Foundation, The Elizabeth George Foundation, The Academy of American Poets, and the Pushcart Prize.

About the Artist

The front and back covers of this book feature paintings by artist Suchitra Mattai, a collaborator who also provided work for a 2018 release, *Chlorosis*. Mattai is a multi disciplinary artist who lives and works in Denver, Colorado. Suchitra was born in Guyana, South America, but has also lived in Halifax and Wolfville, Nova Scotia, Philadelphia, New York City, Minneapolis, and Udaipur, India. These diverse natural and cultural environments have greatly influenced her work and research. While her practice includes a wide range of materials and ideas, her primary interests include 1) the complex relationship between the natural and artificial worlds and 2) the questioning of historical and authoritative narratives, especially those surrounding colonialism. Through painting, fiber, drawing, collage, installation, video, and sculpture, she weaves narratives of "the other," invoking fractured landscapes and reclaiming cultural artifacts (often colonial and domestic in nature).

Suchitra received an MFA in Painting and Drawing and an MA in South Asian art, both from the University of Pennsylvania, Philadelphia. She has exhibited her work in Philadelphia, New York City, Washington, DC, Minneapolis, Denver, Austin, Berlin, London, and Wales, and her work has appeared in various publications such as The Daily Serving (Maile Hung), New American Paintings, and will be in a forthcoming book, "A Collection of Contemporary Women's Voices on Guyana," (Grace Anezia Ali, Brill Press). Her next projects include a large scale commission for the Sharjah Biennial(2019), group exhibitions with the Museum of the Americas, Washington, DC, Pen and Brush, New York, NY, and the Lancaster Museum of Art and History, Lancaster, CA. Recent projects include commissions with the Denver Art Museum/SkyHouse, the Museum of Contemporary Art Denver, and solo exhibitions at the Center for Visual Art, Metropolitan State University Denver (2018), K Contemporary Gallery (2018), Denver, and GrayDuck Gallery, Austin (2018). She recently completed a residency at RedLine Contemporary Art Center, Denver, and is represented by K Contemporary Gallery Denver, and GrayDuck Gallery, Austin.

Mattai writes: *In my practice, land is a conceptual space for the exploration of identity. The places I create are born from memory, history and imagination. Land can offer sanctuary or peril, sometimes both simultaneously. Through installations, mixed media drawings and paintings, collages, and video, I explore how our natural environment(s) shapes personal narratives, ancestral histories and constructions of "self." I want my work to be both intimate and vast. Landscape allows me a wide visual lens within which to situate intimate cultural artifacts and discuss the inextricably intertwined relationship of history and identity. Combining fragments of landscape, vintage objects (often domestic), and culturally specific patterns, I create a nonlinear dialogue with the past. My current projects investigate the role of land in migrations, assimilations, and the creation of "home."*

Front: *"There's a rain cloud in my garden, if only I had a garden,"* 2017. (Acrylic and gouache on synthetic paper, 27"x19.5")

Back: *"Plan B,"* 2017. (Acrylic, tape, and gouache on vinyl, 19.5x27.5")

WHY PRINT / DOCUMENT?

The Operating System uses the language "print document" to differentiate from the book-object as part of our mission to distinguish the act of documentation-in-book-FORM from the act of publishing as a backwards-facing replication of the book's agentive *role* as it may have appeared the last several centuries of its history. Ultimately, I approach the book as TECHNOLOGY: one of a variety of printed documents (in this case, bound*) that humans have invented and in turn used to archive and disseminate ideas, beliefs, stories, and other evidence of production.*

Ownership and use of printing presses and access to (or restriction of printed materials) has long been a site of struggle, related in many ways to revolutionary activity and the fight for civil rights and free speech all over the world. While (in many countries) the contemporary quotidian landscape has indeed drastically shifted in its access to platforms for sharing information and in the widespread ability to "publish" digitally, even with extremely limited resources, the importance of publication on physical media has not diminished. In fact, this may be the most critical time in recent history for activist groups, artists, and others to insist upon learning, establishing, and encouraging personal and community documentation practices. Hear me out.

With The OS's print endeavors I wanted to open up a conversation about this: the ultimately radical, transgressive act of creating PRINT /DOCUMENTATION in the digital age. It's a question of the archive, and of history: who gets to tell the story, and what evidence of our life, our behaviors, our experiences are we leaving behind? We can know little to nothing about the future into which we're leaving an unprecedentedly digital document trail — but we can be assured that publications, government agencies, museums, schools, and other institutional powers that be will continue to leave BOTH a digital and print version of their production for the official record. Will we?

As a (rogue) anthropologist and long time academic, I can easily pull up many accounts about how lives, behaviors, experiences — how THE STORY of a time or place — was pieced together using the deep study of correspondence, notebooks, and other physical documents which are no longer the norm in many lives and practices. As we move our creative behaviors towards digital note taking, and even audio and video, what can we predict about future technology that is in any way assuring that our stories will be accurately told – or told at all? How will we leave these things for the record?

In these documents we say:
WE WERE HERE, WE EXISTED, WE HAVE A DIFFERENT STORY

- Elæ [Lynne DeSilva-Johnson], Founder/Creative Director
THE OPERATING SYSTEM, Brooklyn NY 2018

RECENT & FORTHCOMING FULL LENGTH OS PRINT::DOCUMENTS and PROJECTS, 2018-19

2019

Y - Lori Anderson Moseman
Ark Hive-Marthe Reed
I Made for You a New Machine and All it Does is Hope - Richard Lucyshyn
Illusory Borders-Heidi Reszies
A Year of Misreading the Wildcats - Orchid Tierney
We Are Never The Victims - Timothy DuWhite
Of Color: Poets' Ways of Making | An Anthology of Essays on Transformative Poetics - Amanda Galvan Huynh & Luisa A. Igloria, Editors
The Suitcase Tree - Filip Marinovich
In Corpore Sano: Creative Practice and the Challenged* Body - Elae [Lynne DeSilva-Johnson] and Amanda Glassman, Editors

KIN(D)* TEXTS AND PROJECTS

A Bony Framework for the Tangible Universe-D. Allen
Opera on TV-James Brunton
Hall of Waters-Berry Grass
Transitional Object-Adrian Silbernagel

GLOSSARIUM: UNSILENCED TEXTS AND TRANSLATIONS

Śnienie / Dreaming - Marta Zelwan, (Poland, trans. Victoria Miluch)
Alparegho: Pareil-À-Rien / Alparegho, Like Nothing Else - Hélène Sanguinetti (France, trans. Ann Cefola)
High Tide Of The Eyes - Bijan Elahi (Farsi-English/dual-language) trans. Rebecca Ruth Gould and Kayvan Tahmasebian
In the Drying Shed of Souls: Poetry from Cuba's Generation Zero Katherine Hedeen and Víctor Rodríguez Núñez, translators/editors
Street Gloss - Brent Armendinger with translations for Alejandro Méndez, Mercedes Roffé, Fabián Casas, Diana Bellessi, and Néstor Perlongher (Argentina)
Operation on a Malignant Body - Sergio Loo (Mexico, trans. Will Stockton)
Are There Copper Pipes in Heaven - Katrin Ottarsdóttir (Faroe Islands, trans. Matthew Landrum)

2018

An Absence So Great and Spontaneous It Is Evidence of Light - Anne Gorrick
The Book of Everyday Instruction - Chloë Bass
Executive Orders Vol. II - a collaboration with the Organism for Poetic Research
One More Revolution - Andrea Mazzariello
Chlorosis - Michael Flatt and Derrick Mund
Sussuros a Mi Padre - Erick Sáenz
Abandoners - Lesley Ann Wheeler
Jazzercise is a Language - Gabriel Ojeda-Sague
Born Again - Ivy Johnson
Attendance - Rocío Carlos and Rachel McLeod Kaminer
Singing for Nothing - Wally Swist
Walking Away From Explosions in Slow Motion - Gregory Crosby
Field Guide to Autobiography - Melissa Eleftherion

KIN(D)* TEXTS AND PROJECTS

Sharing Plastic - Blake Neme
The Ways of the Monster - Jay Besemer

GLOSSARIUM: UNSILENCED TEXTS AND TRANSLATIONS

The Book of Sounds - Mehdi Navid (Farsi dual language, trans. Tina Rahimi
Kawsay: The Flame of the Jungle - María Vázquez Valdez (Mexico, trans. Margaret Randall)
Return Trip / Viaje Al Regreso - Israel Dominguez; (Cuba, trans. Margaret Randall)

for our full catalog please visit:
https://squareup.com/store/the-operating-system/

deeply discounted Book of the Month and Chapbook Series subscriptions
are a great way to support the OS's projects and publications!
sign up at: http://www.theoperatingsystem.org/subscribe-join/

DOC U MENT
/däkyəmənt/

First meant "instruction" or "evidence," whether written or not.

noun - a piece of written, printed, or electronic matter that provides information or evidence or that serves as an official record
verb - record (something) in written, photographic, or other form
synonyms - paper - deed - record - writing - act - instrument

[*Middle English, precept, from Old French, from Latin documentum, example, proof, from docre, to teach; see dek- in Indo-European roots.*]

Who is responsible for the manufacture of value?

Based on what supercilious ontology have we landed in a space
where we vie against other creative people in vain pursuit
of the fleeting credibilities of the scarcity economy, rather than
freely collaborating and sharing openly with each other
in ecstatic celebration of MAKING?

While we understand and acknowledge the economic pressures and fear-mongering
that threatens to dominate and crush the creative impulse, we also believe that
now more than ever we have the tools to relinquish agency via cooperative means,
fueled by the fires of the Open Source Movement.

Looking out across the invisible vistas of that rhizomatic parallel country
we can begin to see our community beyond constraints,
in the place where intention meets
resilient, proactive, collaborative organization.

Here is a document born of that belief, sown purely of imagination and will.
When we document we assert. We print to make real, to reify our being there.
When we do so with mindful intention to address our process,
to open our work to others, to create beauty in words in space,
to respect and acknowledge the strength of the page
we now hold physical, a thing in our hand,
we remind ourselves that, like Dorothy:
we had the power all along, my dears.

THE PRINT! DOCUMENT SERIES
is a project of
the trouble with bartleby
in collaboration with
the operating system

www.ingramcontent.com/pod-product-compliance
Lightning Source LLC
Chambersburg PA
CBHW030117100526
44591CB00009B/431